A Southern Panther

A Southern Panther

Conversations with Malik Rahim

Edited by James R. Tracy

A Southern Panther: Conversations with Malik Rahim
Legacy Left Books, an imprint of AK Press
© 2025 James R. Tracy
This edition © 2025 Legacy Left and AK Press
Contributors retain the rights to their individual interviews.

ISBN 9781849356107
E-ISBN 9781849356114
Library of Congress Number: 2024949079

AK Press
370 Ryan Avenue #100
Chico, CA 95973
United States
www.akpress.org

AK Press
33 Tower St.
Edinburgh EH6 7BN
Scotland
www.akuk.com

Cover design by John Yates, www.stealworks.com
Cover portrait by Julianna Sangalang
Legacy Left logo designed by Karina Morera, karinamoreradesign.com
Printed in the USA on acid-free paper

Contents

Introduction 1

Carrying Theory into Practice
Interview with Malik Ismai. 15

Hopesick: The Politics of Housing in an Illiberal City
Conversation with the Whispered Media Collective and
James R. Tracy. 25

Won't Back Down: Malik Rahim and the Fight for the Angola 3
Interview with Jessica Gingrich 51

Finding Common Ground
Interview with James R. Tracy. 73

Climate Justice and the Prisoners' Struggle Go Together
Interview with Mansa Musa 103

Further Reading 121

Acknowledgments. 125

Malik Rahim outside of Common Ground Relief headquarters.
Credit: Todd Sanchioni

Introduction

> We have a saying in my community that when an elder makes his transition without passing down his life experiences, to the next generation, a library has just been burned. I truly believe that those who have lived their lives for peace and environmental justice have a responsibility to make sure that their libraries don't turn to ashes.
>
> —*Malik Rahim*

Malik Rahim's small front porch serves many purposes. Some days, it is a history classroom. Activists and organizers from New Orleans and beyond visit to hear Rahim share his own story, always in the context of the long arc of the Black Freedom Movement. He connects, compares, and contrasts movements from across the decades. Neighbor after neighbor visits for job leads, counseling, hellos, and the news of the day. He makes time for the unending stream of journalists, scholars, students, young activists, and the occasional rock star but most importantly his neighbors. Mostly people he has known since childhood, and who served in the New Orleans Black Panther Party for Self Defense with him.

On the porch with Malik, you realize how grounded his politics are in his immediate community. On the porch, the often-repeated Malian saying about libraries turning to ashes sounds like he had originated it. It is not unusual to sit with Rahim on the porch, and in the middle of an interview, someone else comes by ready to interview him. It is unlikely that his library will turn to ashes.

I first met him in the Spring of 1995 at the end of a rally to support Mumia Abu-Jamal in San Francisco. The usual gauntlet of socialist newspaper sellers, panhandlers, and pamphleteers lined United Nations Plaza. Cutting through the collage of revolutionary slogans, I heard Malik's baritone, "Don't let the San Francisco Housing Authority frame two innocent men!" Standing next to him was Jeff Branner. The two innocent men in question were in front of me. The organization I was a part of, Eviction Defense Network (EDN), had organized a solidarity campaign with residents of public housing facing down the demolition of their homes through the federal Housing Opportunities for People Everywhere (HOPE VI) program. I didn't need to be convinced. We were already aware of the dirty tricks that this city could play with those standing in the way of development deals. I stopped and introduced myself, and quickly found myself a part of Rahim and Branner's defense committee.

Both men had been hired by the San Francisco Housing Authority to help conduct "resident outreach" to support the HOPE VI program. When they realized that they were expected to help residents become comfortable with their own displacement, they quit. True to Rahim's Panther roots he started organizing against the plan. The Housing Authority was having none of it, and soon the pair faced breaking and entering charges for simply trying to retrieve their own records from the Tenant Association office.

Organizing like this can earn one all sorts of prizes from the establishment. Soon after their arrest, local newspapers wrote a series of articles that could only be described as the Willie Hortonization of housing activism. Playing up both of their previous convictions, *The San Francisco Examiner* declared that "Ex-cons Take Over S.F. tenant group." A local television station, KTVU ran a three-part series on the controversy, never once departing from the official script. Neither had ever hid their past. Rahim had completed an armed robbery sentence, and Branner was a former cocaine dealer. Those details only began to matter to the Housing Authority when the pair encouraged residents to question the plan and organize for redevelopment without displacement.[1]

Their defense committee consisted of Marie Harrison of the *San Francisco Bay View* newspaper, Luis Talamantez (a former San Quentin Six compatriot of George Jackson),

---

1. Leslie Goldberg, "Ex-cons Take Over S.F. Tenant Group," *San Francisco Examiner*, February 21, 1995.

Dick Becker, and Gloria La Riva of the Workers World Party. Someone on the committee, I don't remember who, had the brilliant idea of asking William Kunstler, the famed Chicago 7 attorney, to announce that he was coming to San Francisco to defend Malik and Jeff. Kunstler never intended to appear but allowed the word to get out that he was coming for a legal rumble. The charges were unceremoniously dropped. It was a rare moment when playing a bluff card worked.

Rahim never hesitated to share history, strategies, skills, criticism, and praise of our tenant organizing work. The EDN gained a mentor, and I a friend. He is the type of movement elder who will swear up and down that he is quitting organizing. Then he'll switch to talking about the organizing he is actually doing today: the Mutual Aid meeting he just attended, the Land Trust he hopes to establish in Algiers, the young people he is mentoring.

Malik Rahim (born Donald Guyton) was born in 1948 in New Orleans and lives in the Algiers neighborhood where he was raised. Algiers Point was one of the places where enslaved Africans were placed before sale. Visiting William Burroughs in Algiers in 1949, Jack Kerouac described Algiers as "Smoky New Orleans receded on one side; old, sleepy Algiers with its warped woodsides bumped us on the other. Negroes were working in the hot afternoon, stoking the ferry furnaces that burned red and made our tires smell."[2] A short ferry ride away from the French Quarter, today it is a quiet mixed class neighborhood, showing the signs of gentrification.

One of five children, he described his teenage self as a "knucklehead," one of five children. "I brought a lot of grief instead of pleasure to my parents." When he was fourteen, he met Stokely Carmichael and H. Rap Brown when they arrived in New Orleans in 1962 as part of the Student Nonviolent Coordinating Committee witnessing desegregation sit-ins in New Orleans led by Oretha Castle Haley and Rudy Lombard. The movement helped Rahim place the everyday injustices of racism and segregation. He recalls not being able to attend a state-of-the art school, a block from his childhood home, due to segregation.[3]

Seeking a way out of New Orleans, Rahim joined the United States Navy where he connected the racism of home with imperialism abroad. "The next thing I know I'm in Vietnam, and I'm seeing there new types of racism but this time as not a victim of it but a participant. And then I swore that I would never do anything like this again. Cause I watch individuals demonize a people."[4]

Rahim was eventually given a discharge from the military. His growing political consciousness had made him

2. Jack Kerouac, *On the Road* (New York: Penguin, 2003), 141.
3. "Oral History Interview with Malik Rahim," Pamela Hamilton, The Long Civil Rights Movement: The South Since the 1960s. Southern Oral History Program Collection (U-0252) May 23, 2006, https://docsouth.unc.edu/sohp/U-0252/U-0252.html.
4. Ibid.

unfit for military duty. Returning to New Orleans, he was recruited into the National Committee to Combat Fascism, organized in part by another Vietnam Veteran and Louisianian, Geronimo Ji-Jaga Pratt. Building a sizable membership in a short time, the group that would shortly become a new Panther project did what Panthers do: organize free breakfasts, literacy classes, and the containment of the drug trade in public housing.[5]

This earned the newly minted New Orleans chapter of the Black Panther Party the animosity of the State. Across the nation, the Federal Bureau of Investigation, in collusion with local authorities systematically dismantled the Panther project. The Panthers offered the United States an opportunity to confront a history of stolen land, stolen labor, and stolen dreams. Instead, it acted like empires usually do. With a barrage of bullets, a deluge of disinformation, and a mighty payroll—the terror that had already claimed the lives of Chicago Panthers Fred Hampton and Mark Clark would soon visit New Orleans.[6]

This brought Rahim into direct confrontation with the Dixiecrat state. On September 25, 1970, a partnership

---

5. Much of what is remembered about the New Orleans Black Panther Party is due to the groundbreaking work of Orissa Arend. See, Orissa Arend, *Showdown in Desire, the Black Panthers Take a Stand in New Orleans*, (Fayetteville: University of Arkansas Press, 2009).

6. There are many good books about COINTELPRO's impact on the Panthers. One of the best places to start is, Jeffrey Hass, *The Assassination of Fred Hampton: How the FBI and the Chicago Police Murdered a Black Panther* (Chicago: Chicago Review Press, 2019).

between the New Orleans Police Department and the Louisiana State Police began a showdown with the Panthers. The showdown was the second armed conflict between the police and Panthers that month. The Panthers had set up operations in the Desire housing project in the 9th Ward. Governor John McKeithen, widely praised for keeping the peace in tumultuous times, never-the-less supported the raid, vowing to not allow the Panthers to gain a foothold in the state. Fifty years later, revelations showed his method for doing so. Bullets and arrests for Black revolutionaries, and cash payments (in exchange for keeping the lid on violence) for the Ku Klux Klan.[7]

Fourteen Panthers, including Rahim were arrested in Desire after a prolonged battle. Charged with attempted murder of five policemen, the Panthers faced up to twenty years in prison. The prosecution alleged that they were guilty of all manner of mayhem and arson. The defense upheld that the Panther's gunfire was an act of self-defense.[8] Judge Israel M. Augustine Jr. (the first Black judge to preside over a Panther trial) instructed the jury that a guilty verdict was only possible if it could be proven that each defendant was guilty

---

7. Harold Lee Bethune, "14 Arrested in Shoot-Out with the Police, Black Community is Victim of Reign of Terror, 1 Life Lost," *Louisiana Weekly*, September 19, 1970. Also, WWL Staff, "McKeithen Arranged KKK payments to keep peace," WWLTV, April 25, 2016, https://www.wwltv.com/article/news/local/mckeithen-arranged-kkk-payments-to-keep-peace/289-152922706.
8. Roy Reed, "Panthers Freed in New Orleans," *New York Times*, August 7, 1971.

of a criminal act. The jury, of ten Black men and two white men, unanimously acquitted the Panthers on all charges.

While awaiting trial, Rahim and the others were housed in death row of the Orleans Parish Prison. Under normal circumstances residency there would only be possible following a murder conviction. The State's permanent animosity toward Black revolutionaries made this anything but normal circumstances. He has remained in the fight to free political prisoners and to end the death penalty. In the 1980s, he was a founding member of Pilgrimage for Life, along with Sister Helen Prejean which continues anti-death penalty activism to this day as the Louisiana Coalition for Alternatives to the Death Penalty. He also cofounded the International Committee to Free the Angola 3, where he worked tirelessly to exonerate Albert Woodfox, Herman Wallace, and Robert King Wilkerson. The three men formed a chapter of the Black Panther Party within the walls of the Louisiana State Penitentiary at Angola. Prison officials fabricated murder charges against them. Having entered Angola on robbery charges, they gained murder convictions of life without parole.[9] The three were held in solitary confinement for over three decades. Rahim's natural coalition building skills combined with the work of others who took on legal, fundraising, and political support. King was released in 2001 and Woodfox was finally released from prison in 2016.

---

9. Scott Fleming, "Lockdown at Angola. The Case of the Angola 3," in *Liberation, Imagination and the Black Panther Party*, Kathleen Cleaver and George Katsiaficas, eds. (New York: Routledge, 2001).

Wallace was released in 2013 only to die a few days later. King continues to work with Rahim in Algiers to establish a center to welcome formerly incarcerated people home. Woodfox died in 2022. Both men authored powerful memoirs in the best tradition of prison literature.[10]

Common Ground

Common Ground still remains one of the most ambitious mutual aid efforts in the history of the United States. It was founded on Rahim's porch by Sharon Johnson, scott crow, and Robert King in 2005 after Hurricane Katrina. Drawing over 20,000 volunteers from across the globe, the group supported New Orleanians struggling to rebuild their lives as they sorted through the disaster. Common Ground created health clinics, food programs, environmental remediation, and education. They experimented with applying ideas such as democratic decision-making, self-determination, and nonreliance on the state to get things done. On a practical level, Common Ground's volunteers assisted residents in the gutting of houses, roof repairs, and mold removal. It has often been said that Common Ground did what it did because of the absence of the state. This is only half-true. The

---

10. Robert Hillary King, *From the Bottom of the Heap: The Autobiography of Black Panther Robert Hillary King* (Oakland: PM Press, 2009); Albert Woodfox, *Solitary: Unbroken by Four Decades in Solitary Confinement. My Story of Transformation and Hope* (New York: Grove Press, 2019).

state was largely absent from the tasks of relief and repair. It was quite present and active in the business of repression, violence and disaster capitalism. Residents were left to die in the waters of New Orleans. Common Ground mainstay Brandon Darby was later revealed to be a government infiltrator as well as affiliated with several far-right think tanks.[11] Neglect enabled law enforcement and white militias to run campaigns of violence and intimidation against the population.[12] Finally, the tragedy empowered the city to complete the destruction of the public housing where Rahim had lived, worked, defended, and organized throughout his life.

Rahim has always shown his ability to draw from myriad movement organizing traditions. He is rooted in the politics of Black self-determination passed down through his grandparents, who were Garveyites. His work also reflects the ethos of multiracial coalition building that brought the First Rainbow Coalition together. Deeply influenced by the Third World politics that shaped the Panthers, a vast majority of his organizing projects promote a sense of direct democracy and self-management more often associated with the anarchist tradition.

A through line in much of Rahim's work is Intercommunalism, as first articulated through the writings of Huey P.

---

11. Lisa Fithian, "FBI Informant Brandon Darby: Sexism, Egos, and Lies," *The Rag Blog*, March 22, 2010, https://www.theragblog.com/lisa-fithian-fbi-informant-brandon-darby-sexism-egos-and-lies.
12. scott crow, *Black Flags and Windmills: Hope, Anarchy and the Common Ground Collective* (Oakland: PM Press, 2014).

Newton. The theory questioned rigid forms of revolutionary nationalism by arguing that corporations had whittled nations down to small communities that served an imperial center. To shift from this form of reactionary intercommunalism towards a revolutionary one, localized liberated zones must be established. Said Newton, "We see very little difference in what happens to a community here in North America and what happens to a community in Vietnam. We see very little difference in what happens, even culturally, to a Chinese community in San Francisco and a Chinese community in Hong Kong. We see very little difference in what happens to a Black community in Harlem and a Black community in South America, a Black community in Angola and one in Mozambique. We see very little difference."[13]

This approach can be found throughout Common Ground's short history, built from the flooded streets of New Orleans but in direct dialogue with collectives across the globe. In Rahim, intercommunalism sits next to the internationalism that Newton sought to critique. He has often traveled to support governments who are in the crosshairs of U.S. aggression, such as Iraq.

---

13. Huey P. Newton, "Revolutionary Intercommunalism," speech at Boston College, November 18, 1970, https://abolitionnotes.org/huey-p-newton/revolutionary-intercommunalism-1970.

I had an agenda when I arrived on Rahim's porch in May of 2022. My list of questions spanned his entire life. Originally intending to cowrite a biography, health and other unforeseen situations made a change of course necessary. His life and lessons can't be contained in a single pocketbook of interviews, but I hope that *A Southern Panther* will inspire many other efforts to document his life and times.

Rahim made it clear from the start that he wanted us to focus on Common Ground. As an interviewer, I did the best I could to pull out Common Ground's connections to Panther politics, the recurring nightmare of government disruption, the ethos of intercommunalism, and his attempt at once again bringing another coalition together to save the city he loves. I hope that our conversation "Finding Common Ground," adds additional insight to our understanding of this perilous and important time.

This project has grown to include other interviewers. It is fitting that the book starts off with Rahim's conversation with Malik Ismail. In "Carrying Theory Into Practice," he brings out many of the major themes of Rahim's life—including his family's multigenerational commitment in the Black Freedom Movement. I first met Jessica Gingrich when she showed up during one of my interview sessions, ready for her interview with Malik. Since I wasn't done yet, I was only momentarily annoyed. Any consternation I had quickly disappeared as I observed the way she listened to Rahim, as they reflected on the importance of the Angola 3 campaign. Much of the Angola 3 story has been told through the excellent biographies of Albert Woodfox and Robert King, but

Gingrich's contribution, "Won't Back Down: Malik Rahim and the Fight For the Angola 3," serves as a powerful document of long-term solidarity and political principle. I'm grateful to my friends Jeff Taylor and Mark Liiv, formerly of the filmmaking collective Whispered Media for helping to locate and digitalize the long-lost interview, "Hopesick: The Politics of Housing In An Illiberal City." The history of the demolition of the housing safety net in the United States is still woefully under-documented. I'd argue that the HOPE VI program still represents one of the nation's most serious missed opportunities to advance racial and economic justice. Displacement was never inevitable. All that was needed was to implement many of the common-sense proposals advanced by Rahim and public housing residents nationwide. Finally, Mansa Musa ties it all together in "Climate Justice and the Prisoners' Struggle Go Together," originally published by the Real News Network.

Malik Rahim never stopped being a Black Panther. He is a radical organizer whose politics always begin on his porch, in his neighborhood, and with his neighbors. One of the constant themes of this book is his conflicted feelings toward organizing, saying that if he had to do it over again, he would not. Yet, he's never stopped, either. Just days before this manuscript was complete, I received a phone call from him. He and his comrades had just secured a building in Algiers, which they will be developing into a Community Center modeled after the Panther Survival Programs. In what should come as a surprise to no one, Rahim continues to serve the people, five decades after he joined the Party.

Malik Rahim speaks to the press at Common Ground Relief headquarters. Credit: Credit: Todd Sanchioni

Carrying Theory Into Practice
Interview With Malik Ismail

This interview was conducted in October 2023, at the beginning of the 53rd Anniversary Celebration of the founding of the New Orleans Black Panther Party for Self-Defense. Originally broadcast as part *The Vanguard Show*, a podcast of Black Power Media, it has been lightly edited.

Malik Ismail: I am here with Brother Malik Rahim of the New Orleans Chapter of the Black Panther Party, cofounder of Common Ground here in New Orleans. We're on-site in New Orleans. He's a historian and really a New Orleans and Louisiana treasure. And I first met you when we were in Oakland, the fiftieth anniversary, on the steps of Alameda County Courthouse.

And you gave me a big hug. I didn't know if you even knew who I was, but I knew who you were. And again, thank you for sitting down talking with us.

Malik Rahim: It's been an honor.

MI: Yeah, it's definitely an honor as well. And tell us what's going on this weekend.

MR: We are celebrating the fifty-seventh anniversary of the Black Panther Party. It's the fifty-third anniversary of the Louisiana chapter. But it's the fifty-seventh of the national. Fifty-seven years ago, Huey P. Newton and Bobby Seale came together and formed the Black Panther Party, and that's what we are celebrating. We're celebrating the Panther legacy, and at the same time that we are celebrating its rich history, we are also working to dispel the myths in Louisiana about the Black Panther Party.

So, we have what *they* call Black Pantherism. They said that we was a racist organization that was created to kill all white folks. And that we needed to be stamped out. And ever since then, that has been the policy of Louisiana, the neutralization of the party. We want people to know at this celebration the good that the party has done. When we had our shootout, it was a twenty-minute shoot-in. Because we had over one hundred police with long guns shooting at us. And they shot at us for twenty minutes.

MI: This is in the Desire Housing Projects

MR: Yes, in the Desire Housing Projects.

MI: Now, I was going to say, just to backtrack a little bit, how did you grow up? Because I know you're from Algiers. I'm familiar with that area. And how did you grow up? And then, how did you get knowledge on the Black Panther Party at all?

MR: Oh, well, the community that I came up in, we call Algiers, it was once known as Freetown. My grandfather, who I knew, was a World War I veteran. He was in the Universal Negro Improvement Association. Yes. So, I came up in the community of Garveyites and Maroons. My grandmother not only was she a follower of Marcus Garveyites, but she was also a follower of Bishop Henry Turner.

MI: Henry McNeal Turner?

MR: Yeah!

MI: In an African Church, right? After the Methodist Church, right?

MR: I grew up with that spirit, that aroma of civic responsibility. Based upon being rooted in our culture.

MI: And when did you first hear about Huey and Bobby forming the party, or what year did you join, was it a year or two after?

MR: I first heard about the party in '66. Because when they formed the party was shortly after the riots had happened in Los Angeles. I was in the service when the Watts riots happened. When the Magnificent Montague came on [the radio station] KGFJ. He's digging it, and saying, "Well, L.A. is on fire. Burn, baby, burn." So, that's when I found out about the Party. That's, when my conscience started up. I was in boot camp when the Honorable Malcolm X was here. So, I had that history. When Vietnam, I learned that Vietnamese, that the proper name of them, for those people, wasn't gooks. Because that's all we referred to them as, gooks.

MI: Right. U.S. propaganda.

MR: Yeah. And it took a brother to pull me to the side and say, "Man, listen. Every time you're saying gooks, that's like them calling us niggers." So, I don't degrade anybody else. So, with that, after I got out of the service, I stayed in LA. And I was on, what was that, Broadway in 73rd Street in LA. Then I met my first wife. She was going to Fremont High School. So, I started going to Fremont with her. And I met Ron Karenga when he was formulating the US Organization. And he was putting together a plan for Kwanzaa. So, I was seeing the greatness of it because at that time, US and the Panther Party was in the same building.[1]

MI: At UCLA, right?

MR: Yeah. So, again, I watched that grow. But I didn't stay in California because then you had to be twenty-one to go into a nightclub. I've been to Vietnam, everywhere else, doing whatever I want. And now you're going to tell me I got a restriction? So, I left and went back to New Orleans. But I told Geronimo Ji-Jaga Pratt, who was from Louisiana, out there in Morgan City who I had met while I was there, that if they started anything in Louisiana, I'd be there. As soon as I found out that a brother was organizing in New Orleans, I went. My wife and I returned as a family. I had two kids; we were the first family to join the Louisiana Chapter of the Black Panther Party.

MI: Okay. I had the honor to meet Sister Francois. When

1. The US Organization later became a rival to the Black Panther Party. The rivalry, combined with direct counterintelligence operations from the Los Angeles Police Department led to a shootout between the US Organization and the Panthers. This claimed the lives of Alprentice "Bunchy" Carter and John Huggins. See, Laura Pulido, *Black, Brown, Yellow, and Left: Radical Activism in Los Angeles*, (Berkeley: University of California Press, 2006), 99–105.

she came out to Atlanta. Boko, Charles Boko Freeman, and she had an event that I was helping him with, in Atlanta. Tell us about some of your comrades in the chapter.

MR: Well, you talked about one of the greatest. Because, after the first shootout, any individuals that said that they was going to be there for the reopening of the office and make sure that everything continued, they disappeared. Some of them we ain't seen for thirty years, she opened up the office. They went in the office after the police finally got through rampaging and tearing everything up. They went in there. And the residents of public housing. The brothers and sisters from public housing.

They brought us into the project. And we was in a house right adjacent to the project. They brought us into the project and helped us take an abandoned building and turn it into our second office. They cleaned it up and made it our second office. I tell everyone, that we had two National Committees to Combat Fascism. We had the first that was started by a brother named Steve Green and Ryan Ellsworth. And then we had the second one that was started by Aldea Francois and Benny Powell. And they was a part of the second one then. And from the time of the first shootout, where the police, they came on us in a big old armored car. A month later, the city of New Orleans said that it was broke. They didn't have any money for social upliftment programs. But they came up with enough money to buy a tank![2]

2. National Committee to Combat Fascism was the name of the pre-Panther formation in Louisiana. Organized largely by Geronimo

MI: Yeah. That's right.

MR: So, they came to attack our office with a tank. And put us out by surrounding our abandoned building. But the community surrounded our office and wouldn't let them come in. And as I used to always say the wildebeest is at the water hole. But now the wildebeest ain't running away again. They don't know what to do because they're only used to attacking the wildebeest from behind. So now they not showing their behind!

And so now what you going to do? They couldn't come in. What they done, they borrowed some priest uniforms from Loyola University. They came in dressed as priests on Thanksgiving morning. And raided the office. And that's when Benny Toussaint was shot. That was the only member of the party down here to be wounded as a member.

MI: Tell me more about Common Ground because you're one of the cofounders. Common Ground and then Katrina because you had such a visible presence during Katrina in terms of people going through genocide with the police and other residents that were shot at as they tried to seek refuge.

Ji-Jaga Pratt, most of the NCCF members became members of the New Orleans Black Panther Party. This was part of a larger process initiated by the Panthers to gather progressive and revolutionary forces together to combat repression and the growth of far-right reaction. Amy Sonnie and James Tracy, *Hillbilly Nationalists, Urban Race Rebels, and Black Power—Updated and Revised: Interracial Solidarity in 1960s–70s New Left Organizing* (New York: Melville House, 2021) xxvi–xviii.

MR: Well, first I want to say that it wouldn't have been a Common Ground if it wouldn't have been Angola 3 Support Committee. And it wouldn't have been Angola 3 Support Committee if it wouldn't have been the Black Panther Party. I got to go all the way to the roots. Because you never seen a plant flourish without any roots.

You got to go to the roots. That's why we are here. We want people to know our history. And the history of it is that when we founded Common Ground, everything we did was based upon principles that I was taught as a member of the Black Panther Party. I didn't think that I would ever use those type of experience again in life. But when Katrina happened, that's what I had to rely upon. The teachings of the Black Panther Party. That's the reason why we did a multitude of things. Because with the party, it wasn't about just sitting there being an armchair revolutionist. It was all about establishing programs and meeting the needs of the community.[3]

MI: Carrying theory into practice.

MR: That's right. So again, in the aftermath of Katrina, we did our needs assessment. And once we completed our needs assessment, then we started moving on addressing those needs. We started our health clinic, and shortly after

3. For more on the Panther "Survival Programs" or "Survival Pending Revolution" approach, see: Paul Alkebulan, *Survival Pending Revolution: The History of the Black Panther Party* (Tuscaloosa: University of Alabama Press, 2007), and *Alondra Nelson, Body and Soul: The Black Panther Party and the Fight Against Medical Discrimination* (Minneapolis: University of Minnesota Press, 2011).

we formed Common Ground Relief. Two weeks later, we formed Common Ground Health Clinic. To meet the needs of the people because that was a pressing need. Nobody know or truly understand that didn't experience the aftermath of Katrina, how important health care was. Once we seen how it was, how you cannot survive in a 105° weather without the basics. So again, that's what we moved on. We were going to establish the health clinic. We had our distribution center. Then we opened up our wetland restoration. And our soil remediation program. Then we started doing roofing. Cutting out housing.

And by the time I was finally kicked out of Common Ground, we had served over half a million people. And a multitude of services. But again, just like what happened in the party. It happened in the aftermath of Katrina. I call it the COINTELPRO Katrina style. It came in and it destroyed everything that Common Ground was based upon. Simply because of the fact two members of the Party founded it. So again, these are the things that they did to us. I guess when you look at our infiltrator, I don't even want to give him honor by calling his name.

About Malik Ismail

Malik Ismail is an international writer and revolutionary activist born in Miami, Florida. From an early age he was influenced by Malcom X, Muhammad Ali, and the Black Panther Party, which would impact his life in activism. He is a former Panther Minister of Information in the New Panther Vanguard Movement (formerly known as New

African-American Vanguard Movement) whose writings have been published in The L.A. Watts Times, rolling out Magazine, *It's About Time newsletter,* The Black Panther International News Service. *Ismail has been profiled in* The African Times *and is an Honorary Member of the 1976–1981 Southern California Chapter of the Black Panther Party. He is the host of the podcast* The Vanguard Show.

Malik Rahim addresses Common Ground Relief volunteers.
Credit: Todd Sanchioni

Hopesick

The Politics of Housing in an Illiberal City, Conversation with the Whispered Media Collective and James R. Tracy

Malik Rahim is perhaps best-known for his history as a Panther, a defender of political prisoners, and organizing grassroots relief post-Katrina. Less is known about his work to defend public housing residents in the 1990s. Rahim moved to San Francisco to organize with residents of public housing during the demolition and reconstruction process known as the Housing Opportunities for People Everywhere VI (HOPE VI) program. As administered by the Clinton Administration, HOPE VI promised to reverse decades-long federal housing policies of segregation and concentration of poverty. In the majority of cities, the program resulted in a drastic loss of low-income housing and the displacement of long-term residents. This interview illustrates Rahim's lifelong commitment to residents of public housing, tracing back to the showdown in the Desire projects of New Orleans.

In San Francisco, Rahim and Jeffrey Banner were arrested on dubious charges of breaking and entering into the offices of the Resident Council they had helped to form. For organizing residents to demand the right to return, and the support of Black-led cooperatives, they were subjected to a slanderous media campaign in the local media implying that criminals had taken over the Tenant Association of Bernal Dwellings Public Housing.

This interview was conducted in San Francisco in early 2001 for the film *Boom! The Sound of Eviction*, by Jeff Taylor and A. Mark Taylor (Whispered Media Collective) and James R. Tracy, then a volunteer organizer with the Eviction Defense Network. The majority of the footage landed on the cutting room floor and was not included in the film.

Panther Memories

I learned much of how I organize today in the New Orleans Panthers. I would say the best years of my life was in the Panther party. It was probably the proudest time of my existence. There's no other gratification that I've ever received in life greater than the gratification I received in being in the party and of the experience that I had with individuals in the party. I would say probably every month, at least three-or four-party members was being killed across the country. It formed a real unique bond between us. The true essence of comradeship.

I was involved in a shootout in housing projects of New Orleans. In Louisiana, anytime there was a black insurrection, it was crushed—and by crushed, I mean that the participants in it were killed, were brutally killed. The communities around the city had become like wildebeest, you know how it is when lions come through the wildebeests just run to get away from it. But this was a time that the wildebeests turned around and said we ain't running!

From that day, I've always worked with public housing residents. It was in 1970, and from 1970, there hasn't been a year when I have not organized in public housing. When we were establishing the Panthers, the governor of the state had warned that he wasn't going to let us get established. Every time we would get an office, we would be served with eviction orders and kicked out. We decided that once we got to Desire, because most of us was from public housing, that's where we was going to make our stand. That was the worst public housing development in the city of New Orleans at that time.

We decided that was the development that we was going to transform. It was a community that had little or no hope. The average annual income at that time of a resident of public housing was around $1,200 to $1,500 a year, and crime was rampant. When we went into Desire, we went into that to show exactly what the Black Panther Party could do. And again, at that time, even up to today, this nation, this country, this government have never been in the business of eliminating poverty. It's always been how we're going to maintain poverty, just to keep it going, keep it going smoothly from those who kind of kick up too many waves.

There's places for us. There's prisons. There's the graveyard. Poor Blacks have always been considered in this nation as a cancer. And there's only three things you do with a cancer. Either you kill it, you drug it, or you cut it out. And with us, it's always been easy. They would kill us. Our community, even today is inundated with drugs. And to cut us off, you just look at the prisons and jails.

That's always been this country's means of dealing with us. The year of 1970 was a unique year. It was a year that at that time, President Nixon had decided that, hey, Blacks was becoming too educated. The move was then to eliminate Blacks going to colleges and public housing. Whites were leaving the projects and they were being filled with more Blacks. You see that whole transformation in every other county that I came from of who was those that was placed in those positions. So that's what kicked my involvement off into it.

Displacement in an Illiberal City

You have to look back in history. As an African American, the only thing I could look at is what happened to the Native Americans. Gentrification was what happened here when gold was found in the hills of California, which meant elimination and a total genocidal movement for the extermination of Native Americans, that's what it has always represented.

I haven't seen liberal San Francisco. I've only seen conservative San Francisco. There's no way that I could say that in a liberal community or a progressive community, the things that have happened over the last eight years that I've been in this city never could have happened in a progressive city, so I could never classify it as a progressive or liberal city. Look what happened. It didn't happen only in the Mission District. It happened and it didn't only happen to African Americans, that's all you got to do is look at the history of Chinatown, Japantown, so what happened to us was just a continuation of that form of racism. And now, so much of that racism is carried out by people who share my skin color.

I have to say, which I tell anybody, I believe Mayor Willie Brown is the worst type of grifter. He's a grifter and that's a person that don't care about nothing but themselves and he epitomized that word. Why am I saying that? It is because he sold out his people. People had hope in him and he literally just sold us out just to become mayor. In the 1930s, there was a movie that was done, James Cagney starred in it and the name of it was "What Price Glory?," it was about World War I, that era and it was this person, Sergeant Flag, who wanted to get this woman, and for what price he would pay for and the things that was going on.

Same thing happened to Mayor Brown, but to a greater extent and what I mean by that, to become mayor, he literally gave away Black communities, he made sure that these communities was given away to developers, to support him as becoming mayor and then in the interim, he duped Blacks in the city by believing that it was going to be a Black thing and he was going to turn around and what kind of prosperity he was going to bring to the communities and that's all you got to do is look around. More Blacks have left the city than stayed in the city, more Black communities have been literally destroyed and taken away than have seen any type of prosperity, more Blacks are being arrested, more Blacks are being sent to prison, more Blacks are being forced to live butchered, half-starved lives in a city that, everywhere you look, you see prosperity.

It becomes a Black thing to him when he could benefit from it. But when he finds no benefits in it, it's all about that green. It's all about making money. I mean, look at him. He came here as a poor person, came to public housing. When he first moved to this city, he was in public housing as a poor Black man with nothing. No other Black could look for that type of salvation today. No other Black could say that, hey, if I leave that south, if I leave the racism in the south to come out west because I heard there were opportunities in California, they cannot find a place to stay in here. Now they can't find the opportunities that he took advantage of if they no longer exist. The only thing they could find is a prison cell because now that's public housing in the state of California.[1]

Prisons, just look at them. Most of the work I do is on prisons. In California, almost 70% to 80% of African Americans that are in prison came out of public housing, whether it's public or Housing and Urban Development-subsidized housing. Something is wrong when you're talking about that many people coming out of one community. We have spent three times as much on keeping a person in prison as we give

1. See James Richardson, *Willie Brown: A Biography* (Berkeley: University of California Press, 1996).

a person to live in public housing. In one of these housing developments, there's a kid who's under house arrest right now in Hunter's View. If you have a monitor, I believe they spend something like about $55 a day to monitor him. Now his mother is only getting $7,000 a year to raise four kids.

The average lifespan of an African American male is only 59 years, but the lifespan of a white or one of these Willie Brown clones or other so-called, I wouldn't call them Blacks and I wouldn't even call them Negroes, I can't even think of a word to call them. Whites, in the city, their lifespan is basically 76 years. Something is totally wrong when two people could live in the same city, one could look forward to only living 59 years and the other could look forward to living 76 years, something is wrong.

During our organizing around the HOPE VI program, we came up with so many good ideas around positive community economic uplift. That was crushed. And there was the internal corruption. There was a Relocation Specialist who worked for the Housing Authority who we thought was working to ensure that the relocation of residents was done in a humane, dignified manner. He is now in prison for selling Section 8 certificates. We tried to sound the alarm. We did a demonstration in the office of the Housing Authority director, Ronnie Davis. To let him know that this was going on. He didn't care.

We had a lot of programs. A social upliftment program that was established. Bernal was the first housing project to have a Narcotics Anonymous program. The housing authority crushed it. Mayor Brown crushed it. The job training program that was established so that residents could take advantage of the construction opportunities that were awarded under HOPE VI was crushed.

We had a housing painting cooperative. The first time in the history of public housing that a painting cooperative was established by residents for residents of public housing. It was established at Bernal. Look and see who was doing the painting. Know when [Housing Authority] director Ronnie Davis found out that we had established a painting cooperative in this city, he started giving everybody painting jobs. They complied on the surface with demands for local hire. You had journeyman painters that were qualified to be a journeyman painter in public housing but couldn't do painting work for no other job under the union except for in public housing.

And then when you look at the Housing Authority, there are always two authorities, one that's ran by Blacks and one that's ran by whites. And when you look at the one that's ran by whites, that's where the big money is at. That's the construction dollars. The whites have that Housing Authority. The one that's Black was run by Ronnie Davis, who's now indicted. What you find is that you're seeing, as for what's happening in public housing in this city is the biggest crime I've ever seen in this country. If that was is a liberal city, then the liberal community in this city must be lost all they drive or anything, because they sure have been voiceless. As for the plight of their fellow citizens in this city.

HOPE VI promised us something that we all wanted. Finally invest in public housing and fix up those buildings.

But we got something else. I think it was organizer Steve Williams, who first called it "Hopeless" or "Hoax 6." It was supposed to stand for Housing Opportunity for People Everywhere. It was supposed to offer social and economic upliftment for the community along with the revitalization of their community. Not the developers but the community.

In San Francisco, HOPE VI has never shown any type of revitalization or social or economic upliftment for residents. Residents at Hayes Valley, they were only hired for the small length of time and basically as laborers, so they never got any skills. At Bernal and Hayes Valley, and Plaza East it was the same thing. There ain't no hope in it.

Scam Francisco

There were almost 1000 Section 8 certificates that were set aside when the Housing Authority found out about the loophole for the one-for-one replacement of the demolished units. At first, the federal government required a home that is demolished must be replaced. But here was a loophole in the plan. If you give the resident a Section 8 certificate you don't have to replace that unit. The Housing Authority in San Francisco took 1000 certificates and put them aside to help something like about 900 families that were supposed to be in the three developments that were scheduled for demolition under HOPE VI.

Now half of the families stayed in public housing. So that's 500 Section 8 certificates that were left. What happened to them? How could a person who's supposed to be over these Section 8 certificates allow 500 certificates just to get away? When we asked these questions, we was classified as gangsters and troublemakers and everything else.

But they was given carte blanche to sell, evict. They put a lot of people out. Just evict them for anything. That's because the federal government wouldn't require them to pay to relocate an evicted resident. When they evict you, they still had the Section 8 certificates. We had a resident at Bernal Dwellings named Mrs. Long who literally died fighting to save her house. They wanted to evict her because her grandson was arrested with marijuana. Not that he was in the projects doing anything wrong. But they used this minor offense to put out a woman who had never been late in rent, had been living in the projects since the early 60s. She had been a role model for all other residents because every resident that went there basically went to Mrs. Long to find out just to get along in that project.

They literally killed that woman. Her daughter was on crack. She took her grandkids to try to save them. The Housing Authority didn't come to the rescue. They came with an eviction notice because her grandson was arrested. She was literally forced out. It wasn't until we said we were going to expose the selling of those Section 8 certificates they finally did give her a her a voucher. But as soon as they gave it to her, she died. No, it wasn't the revitalization and uplift plan that the Housing Authority had. It was to get those poor individuals out of this valuable property by any means necessary.

You have residents being tossed on the streets for the

simplest violation. If I have a dog, I get kicked out. If I get a gun, I'm kicked out. In America, we have two sets of rules. There's one set of rules for your middle class and your white community, and then you have another set of rules for your poor and your Black community or your minority communities. And your minority communities have no rights.[2]

Decades of Displacement

I didn't live in Fillmore, but when I first came to California was in 1965. I was on my way to Vietnam. I first came in in '65. The first time I experienced San Francisco was in '66 as a serviceman. We were here at Treasure Island. I stayed in San Francisco for maybe two or three days. The first thing I did, as soon as we had liberty (I was in the Navy), was hop on a bus to Fillmore. Why? Because that's all that was known, man. If you come to San Francisco, go to Fillmore. If you're Black, Fillmore is the spot. I spent time there and felt proud to walk down Fillmore and see Black people on both sides of the street owning businesses, I mean, really doing things.

2. In the 1990s, the Congress and the Clinton Administration passed the Housing Opportunity Extension (HOPE Act) which instituted a "One Strike and Your Out!" eviction policy in public housing. Touted as a way to increase safety, it was exploited to reduce the amount of HOPE VI residents eligible for relocation assistance. Often, family members lost their homes for the actions of relatives. See James Tracy, *Dispatches Against Displacement: Field Notes from San Francisco's Housing Wars* (Oakland: AK Press, 2014).

After I got out of the service and after I was in the Panther party, I moved to what is now East Palo Alto. Then it was Palo Alto, and I was involved in the Nairobi Movement.[3] And I was going to Nairobi College then. Every Friday, we would leave from there and come and spend the weekend in San Francisco. I didn't live here, but it was so great to come here to visit, to see, to walk down and see, not people talking about how I'm going to survive by selling drugs but people who were genuinely talking about providing legitimate services to meet the basic needs of their people. And that was going on in the Fillmore at that time.

You had hotels that were owned by Blacks. You had theaters. Some of the best jazz I've ever heard. I heard it here, right there, right there on the Fillmore. But now I see everybody else coming through there. And a lot of times, I walk down Haight, walk down Fell, Oak, or Divisadero. And I say, "Well, Goddamn, how could this happen so quickly and how could so much be lost so quickly without any type of person standing up and saying, 'Well, hey, what has happened is wrong?'" But then I say, *Well, if we live in a country that is governed by a government that never says slavery was wrong, never apologizes to the Indians, the Native Americans, for the injustice*

---

3. The Nairobi Movement was a lesser-known Black Power project in East Palo Alto. It was a grassroots movement that organized for control of local institutions. It was affiliated with the Nairobi College, part of a wave of "Third World" colleges established in the 1960s and 70s. See Mary Eleanor Rhodes Hoover, "The Nairobi Day School: An African American Independent School, 1966–1984," *The Journal of Negro Education* 61, no. 2 (1992): 201–10.

that has been perpetrated against them, so if they could do that, then it becomes understandable why the Fillmore could be lost.[4]

And, man, even if you look at pictures, newsreels, or others about what was happening there, it wasn't nothing. You can't even equate it to how that experience was. Now, you look at Third Street, full of drugs, full of poverty, but it's black, basically, right up in here. And you take this and you look at what Fillmore was, and that was thirty years ago. It's the differences, day and night. The same thing happened to Willie Brown, but to a greater extent. And what I mean by that, to become mayor, he literally gave away Black communities.

When these housing developments were built, most of them were built in the 1940s, the property value in San Francisco was around a national norm. But in the seventies, property value in San Francisco started to increase at a greater rate, at a phenomenal rate in San Francisco and Boston. HOPE VI was a continuation of the old Urban Renewal. The only thing different this time is that during the seventies it was whites doing this to Blacks. Alright, so it was able to unite us. But now you have Blacks doing this to Blacks. So, the little unity that did exist was shattered.

You're looking at property value of a public housing development of over a billion dollars. You're talking about

4. For background on the destruction of the Fillmore neighborhood see, Rick Butler, "The Fillmore," in *Neighborhoods: The Hidden Cities of San Francisco*, directed by Rick Butler and narrated by Ossie Davis, KQED, 1999.

poor people living on property with a value of over a billion dollars in this city. It caused these avaricious businessmen and developers to say, well, hey, if we remove these people out of here, this is what we could do with this property. With that came concessions. The mayor just kissed ass. Just sold us out. Just sold the communities out so he could go down in history as the first Black mayor of San Francisco. When the mayor says we're going to clean up the neighborhood, he means clean it up. It means just what he says. He's gonna clean up the neighborhood. He didn't bring jobs, opportunities to the community, because he could have. When you look at one contractor who made over $130,000,000 on HOPE VI and three developments, not one.

One developer made over $130,000,000 off one development alone in this city. One contractor, McCormick and Baron proven to have violated every law and covenant in HUD to get that contract for Hayes Valley. But the numbers of the displaced just piled up, they told the feds you know, we know we did wrong, but it's too late. It'll cost too much to get rid of us. So now the same developer who has violated all her laws has gotten all three developments.

Organizing: Bigger than a Paycheck

I would say the first thing that I would tell anyone to do that is a so-called organizer, and that's to be committed. In the last five years, I've never made over $5,000 in any one year.

In the last five years, last year, my income was $2,200. In '99, I made something like about $1,600. When you look at the sacrifice that must be made, those that can, should be able to help others.

I was blacklisted from so many jobs in San Francisco. The Mayor had basically denied me any opportunity of employment in this city. And most others that were so scared of him wouldn't employ me when he said I was a drug dealer, and we were terrifying residents in there.

Then if you're a liberal or you're a progressive, if you're a Christian or Muslim, whatever you are, if you stand for what is right, then you should go in there and say, well, hey, if this is what's going on in this community, then we're going in there and we're going to make sure that it's stopped.

I'd be damned. I'm not sure I would never want any of my kids becoming organizers. I would never allow them to get involved in this type of struggle. Why? I felt like I've paid the ultimate price for them. I believe that they have paid the price of going without. It's a hurting thing for a parent to ever tell his child, "Hey, I can't afford to get you this."

And I have done that for him all his life because he was the last child that was born at Bernal Dwellings housing projects. And from then up until now, that's all he has seen: "My Daddy isn't working. My daddy is unemployed. Daddy, why don't you have a new car like all our neighbors? Why are we shopping at Goodwill?" These things here, and these are the types of sacrifices that I wouldn't ask anybody else to make. Like I told my kids, I made the sacrifice for them, and you made the sacrifice as a child. So hopefully, when you grow up, you don't have to talk about doing this. I continue to do it because this is all I know.

My only income is the 10% veteran benefit that I get, which is $100 a month. I guess the only reason why I'm able to survive is that I have no vices. I don't drink, I don't smoke. I could never tell a person, no community organizer, to get involved in this because I couldn't afford to offer them any type of compensation for the repercussions of their actions if they stand for real righteousness.

The only thing I could tell a person is that this is something that has its highs and lows. The highs are when you see a community being uplifted, and the lows are when you start seeing the government, this government that's supposed to be working with you, being the most oppressive thing that's tearing your community down. If you are committed to the struggle for peace and justice, the first thing that you need to do is unite and be there to assist others. You know, the struggle that I was in, if it wasn't for very few friends now, I'd be in prison.

And I'm basically a single parent, just me and my son. I have a family that's in a position that could help us out, and other than that, it's just money that I could get out here and hustle.

Repression and Community

When Jeff Branner and I were framed up by San Francisco, very few people came to our defense. You [James R. Tracy] were there, a few friends and members of a socialist group, the Workers World Party. But that's what it took. It took the socialists. If it wouldn't have been for them, I know I would be dead. Workers World literally saved my life. Dick Becker, Gloria La Riva. If it wouldn't have been for them, I know they would either have killed me or would have given me life in prison. I'm not a socialist, I'm not a communist, and I'm not a member of Workers World, but I am a staunch advocate for truth. And the truth is that they came out, they were the ones that when nobody else believed. I felt abandoned by my community and had no hope. As for the Black community, the Black churches, or the mosque, and I'm a Muslim, and I'm telling you as a Muslim, the mosque didn't come out, the church didn't come out.

When the *Chronicle* planted that article that Jeff and I were running this project by fear and doubt, none of them came out to find out whether this is true or not. We were just abandoned. It was only a few organizers that basically came out. And you know, we see that this isn't true and we're going to stand by you. We had some connections. We knew [movement attorneys] William Kunstler and Ramsey Clark. And that's what it took. It took a letter from them threatening to come to represent us, to make them drop the charges. It was a bluff card. But it worked. We would be in prison. But then they said that this was in '96, that by the end of that year, Jeff and I were supposed to have been in prison. But now Jeff is a minister, I'm still here. The Police Chief that was running around telling people we were trying to buy the projects with drug money, his ass is gone. The people who wrote letters to

Jeff's Parole Officer, saying he is violating his parole, are now nowhere to be found. Housing Authority Director Ronnie Davis, who sat up there and talked about how we were trying to steal and intimidate residents and he wasn't going to allow us to beat people out of their life. Indicted.

Land and Liberty

It's all about land. How can you have a community without land? All right. How can you have the basics of human life without land? How can you have any type of organized society without land? So, yeah, it's all based upon first water and then land. And then from there, then you could start talking about shelter, clothing, food. But without that, first basics. Life as we know it evolved once we came ashore, once there was land. So, yeah, land is the beginning of everything.

And in a society, because you look at San Francisco, it's also a county, it's the smallest county in the state of California, and it's the only county that is comprised of just one city. And then when you look at this city and why is that? Because of the Financial District. They made sure that it wasn't going to make the mistakes that happened in New York. Other than that, Manhattan would be a city. You would hear about maybe the other boroughs around there but it'd be Manhattan. When they looked at and seeing what happened in New York, they were making sure that they were going to control the power here.

They controlled it by keeping it as one little unified

county. And in this county, when you talk about land, I mean with 49 square miles for a county, not a city, because this would be a small, very small land-wise as a city within a county, but for a county to be 49 square miles. . . . And then when you look at it, look how built up it is. For you to really build now in San Francisco, you have to eliminate something.

Who you want to eliminate? They ain't going to run out nobody with money. They ain't going to allow nobody to run out with influence and power. Who are they going to run out? The poor, the powerless. I could remember in this state that if you had a job, even though it was a mid-level working job, you had the opportunity of buying a home, you had the basics. That opportunity was there. But now if you have a job, you don't even have the opportunity of renting a home, let alone buying. It's so far-fetched now to hear youngsters talking about buying anything that even resembles a home here unless they're selling drugs or either they're kissing ass.

I hear people in my community say, *Malik, what you're saying is true. But lord, I don't want you around me. I don't want anybody to see you talking to me because I don't want any chances of me losing my job and then being tossed out on the street because I'm affiliating with you.*

You have this land as the basics. From land, the opportunities of what's going to be put in this land are great. I hope that if they run all the poor, all the minorities, out of San Francisco, that this motherfucker falls into the ocean. That's what I wish. I wish that as soon as they get all the rich over here that they want here, as soon as they're all here, they have a Black and White Ball and this motherfucker drops into the ocean, drowning all their asses, and they could be known as the lost city of San Francisco. Because that's what they deserve.

I mean, look at it. Right here we have a power plant that is polluting us. We have lead in our water that's retarding our children. Now, we have a navy shipyard with a fire that's been burning for damn near three years. The Navy is telling us, *Yeah, we put it out, but you can't come and check to make sure that it's out.* We have a sewage plant telling us, *Yeah, you can live here as long as we can throw all our waste in your community.* You're talking about a hot day? Come out here on a real hot day when that sewage plant is smelling you up. And then they tell us, *Hey, yeah, we're going to come in here now. We're going to help you all. "Well, man, listen, we're here to close that power plant."*

But every time I ask a lot of them one question, *once it's cleaned up, you're going to help us stay here*? Then the conversation shifts. Who are we going to clean it up for? Who are we going to go through all these changes for? You ain't telling me that you're going to go through it for my son. And I know I would kill if I would find out that my son got cancer because he's forced to breathe in this air in here.

There were very few white public housing advocates, and many of them avoided us and didn't want anything to do with our cause. They knew the laws and were aware of the injustices happening in our community, but they chose not to act. This was because they were still able to rent houses at that time. However, when the same issues started affecting them, they suddenly wanted to come together and discuss solutions.

My response to them has always been, *Fuck you, why should I work with you now? You didn't work with me when my house was on fire. Why should I help put out yours?* And there are many of them. You dig that? I told them then that we were like the canary in a mining shaft. Now, you watched us die. You watched us being ran off. Now your ass is being ran off. But I asked them, oh, where was your motherfucking ass when we asked you to come and help us in public housing? If we could have stopped it then, it wouldn't have gotten this far. But you didn't give a fuck about it because you were living. You were running around on the Haight. You were running on Valencia. You dig? You were drinking your coffee and tea and saying, yeah, it was all wrong, but we don't have time.

American Decline

It's real fucked up when you find that this is the way America has come. Because like I said, I'm 53, I'm on my way out. But then I see kids that are coming up now that even right now in the year 2001 aren't given half of the opportunities that I was afforded. I made a conscious decision based not only on the opportunities that were present, but also the opportunities that I faced. But I see kids now, and they are not faced with those types of choices. I don't know what it's like to have a mother who's on crack. My mother wasn't. That didn't exist. My mother wasn't selling her body to buy drugs.

That didn't exist in my community. I didn't know anything about seeing a person killed until I was twelve years old.

My son is only five, and he has already seen dead bodies. In a white community, when a person dies, they have all types of psychologists and others to help them through the trauma. But here, in a community like ours, there's no support. They feel like, well, either you get used to it, or it's just something you have to deal with. This is what we're talking about. Can it be changed? Sure, it can be changed if American people would understand that the conditions that happen to us can happen to others. I remember the first time I brought up what was happening in this city's public housing to outside activists, and how it was seen as a "Black thing."

Looking Forward, Looking Back

Mayor Brown turned into a full-fledged participant in the destruction of the Black community. At that time, he was poor. Now he is filthy rich. At that time, he wasn't a part of it, but now he's entrenched in it. It's a qualitative difference. It's not quantitative; it's a qualitative difference in his involvement.

Other communities have gotten organized in the past. In the 1970s, the Mission was in a much different situation. Why? Because the Latino community figured out organizing. One is because there were immigrants. You're talking about basically a Latino immigrant community. In a lot of cases, they weren't afforded the opportunity of voting. They didn't have anyone but a few to stand up for them. But those who did knew how to organize.

You know you had great organizers like Richard Sorro. You had others that are now dead. The Mission Coalition Organization. Daniel Hernandez with Mission Housing and Development Corporation. You had individuals that were standing up, and they had the vision, the foresight to see that, hey, we're in a position where we're going to have to make compromises, but we're going to build affordable housing. If we can't get anything else, we are going to keep our people here. We're going to make sure that, as best we can, our people can stay here. That happened at one time in the Black community. That's the reason why you're here at Northridge, this cooperative is here because people stood up.[5]

The reason why even though Jackie Robinson [a subsidized housing development] has now gone to an outside developer, it now has debt. So, I think, if some type of salvage can be done for their community, do I think that there's hope for Mission? I don't think so. I'm a pessimist, so I couldn't tell you that I've only seen defeat. I've always been on the wrong side. I've always been on the losing side. But I don't believe that because you have lost me and you were wrong. Because I've always stood for the right thing. And I believe that those in that community who are struggling need to stand up, they need to understand that if they're going to

---

5. Rahim is referencing the Mission Coalition Organization, one of the few organizations that defeated urban renewal displacement in the 1970s.

save any more of it. Right now, it's not about race, because you have people of color who are getting filthy rich on the destruction of that community. You have so-called Blacks and so-called Latinos. Because I believe any person who will sell out their own for a dollar, I don't believe you can even find a definition for that in Webster. But when you have a community where you can label a person disposable, and I feel like when you say, "Because I'm rich, I deserve this," and "Because you're poor, you deserve this," and there's no equity in it, and you'll find that this is what's happening when you're talking about money. That's what it's all about. And if I could rent a house to you and you have ten kids and you're poor, you're not paying my rent on time, and here you come with no kids and want that same house and you're giving me a year's rent in advance, then there goes that family, and no consideration is made on what to do with that family. At Bernal Dwellings, it was a high-rise building. It was a family high-rise building. Eight floors. It was a complete failure. But high-rise senior citizen housing has been a success. That was sixty-four units that could have been set aside for sixty-four seniors that were torn down. So that's sixty-four seniors who now cannot find housing that could have been had there.

So, they could have built more units on that land. They built less. They took 208 units, demolished them to build 164 units in a city where the demand wasn't increasing, but was jumping by leaps and bounds. They said, "Well, yeah, well, we're going to build some new housing, but we're going to build less." The developer who got those three developments, in the next fifty-five years, he's going to make over a billion dollars at present rent. At present rent, he's going to make over a billion dollars in the next fifty-five years on those three developments. When they say business is cold, business is freezing, there's no such thing as any love or consideration. When you find that and you look in that community, just look at it. If you go and rent a place, put a "for rent" sign up on it. You put a "for rent" sign up in the Mission, and you have them coming in droves to rent the place. And it's who has the money. There was a movie that I was watching one day with my son, because a lot of times, we watch a lot of movies. It was a Walt Disney movie, and the genie was an evil genie in the movie. And this guy, who was talking, Jabbar, I believe, was his name, was talking about the golden rule. And he said, "Yes, the golden rule. Those who have the gold make the rules." And that's what it's known. So, when you're talking about the Mission, it's all about money.

About Whispered Media

Whispered Media was a San Francisco film collective that played a critical role in documenting the Global Justice Movement of the 90s and 2000s. In collaboration with other organizations, they produced Reclaim May Day! (1998), Showdown in Seattle: Five Days that Shook the WTO (1999), The Pie's the Limit (1999), Breaking the Bank (2000), *and* Boom! The Sound of Eviction (2001).

Robert Hillary King, Albert Woodfox, and Malik Rahim.
Credit: jackie summell

Won't Back Down

Malik Rahim and the Fight For the Angola 3
Interview with Jessica Gingrich

In this interview with journalist Jessica Gingrich, Malik Rahim recalls the campaign to free Panther comrades Albert Woodfox, Herman Wallace, and Robert Hillary King from solitary confinement at the Louisiana State Penitentiary, or "Angola."

At twenty-eight square miles, Angola is the largest maximum-security prison in the United States. Located a two-hour drive from New Orleans, it was named after Angola Plantation, one of four owned by Isaac Franklin. Known as "America's Bloodiest Prison," it served as a symbol of white supremacy's shift from formal slavery to a carceral Jim Crow regime. Here, Woodfox, Wallace, and King—known as the Angola 3—spent most of their adult lives.

Each of the three men arrived at Angola on separate convictions. King and Wallace joined the Panthers while incarcerated at the Orleans Parish Prison (OPP). Before Angola, Woodfox had come into contact with the New York

Panthers during one of his many escapes from OPP. Together with other prisoners, they founded a prison chapter of the Black Panther Party. The Angola Panthers challenged the prison's culture of violence by protecting vulnerable prisoners and organizing food and work stoppages. They worked to ease racial tensions between Black and white prisoners.

In 1972, Woodfox and Wallace were convicted of the murder of prison guard Brent Miller. King was placed in solitary soon after being transferred to Angola. Prosecutors were unable to produce physical evidence, but they did present testimony from Hezekiah Brown, a prisoner who received preferential housing at Angola in exchange for his testimony.

Rahim's involvement in the Campaign to Free the Angola 3 reflects his lifelong commitment to political prisoners. Mobilizations outside the prison bolstered intense legal work inside courtrooms. The campaign also gained support from Body Shop founder Anita Roddick, who brought the case to Amnesty International's attention. Prominent supporters included artist Rigo 23, Harry Belafonte, and Representative John Conyers.

The case brought attention to the abuse of solitary confinement and ultimately led to the Angola 3's freedom. King was released in 2001 and has remained a steadfast activist in New Orleans. His autobiography, *From the Bottom of the Heap: The Autobiography of a Black Panther,* was published in 2008. He now runs a praline company that funds his activism.

Wallace died in 2013, three days after his release from prison. He wrote prolifically while he was incarcerated and the catalyst for much of the outside support that the three received from outside the prison

Albert Woodfox was released in 2016. His book, *Solitary,* won the Stowe Prize and the Louisiana Endowment for the Humanities Book of the Year. He was a finalist for the Pulitzer Prize and the National Book Award for Nonfiction. He died in 2022.

Algiers

Religion has always played a major part in the African American community that used to exist over here. I'm talking about pre-Betsy. Betsy was in 1965. The hurricane transformed Algiers but all the way up until Betsy, spirituality played a major role for a lot of people ever since the end of the Civil War. A lot of Black veterans from the Civil War founded a lot of the original churches here.

Betsy changed Algiers and the bridge first. It and the bridge are the two things that happened that had the greatest impact upon Algiers. They built that bridge and caused the destruction of one of the oldest African American communities, really, in the South. A lot of people still believe that Treme is the oldest African American community, but I tell them, "Treme is the oldest People of Color community and that's the African community in Algiers so again. . ."

After the bridge was Urban Renewal. All of a sudden Oakdale or Freetown whatever one it was referred to by then was classified as an eye sore and they didn't want people coming across the bridge and the first thing they see is an African ghetto but in that little African ghetto 90% of the people that lived there was homeowners, not homebuyers, but homeowners. They had people there that owned property. Ever since the 1800s some families have lived there so when the hurricane happened, it brought people from down the bayou, the 9th Ward. All the areas that was impacted by the hurricane were going all over to the city and into the Fischer Projects.

You brought people that was impacted, that had just lost everything, and then you pile them up in this brand-new development without any service so it brought crime. It had a real impact on drugs. It overwhelmed our community because at one time you may have had a thousand, not even a thousand African American families that was originally living in Algiers. Now all of a sudden you open up a housing development with over a thousand units so these equal or surpass the existing resident community growth. So, they had—how do you say?—a quality, qualitative impact, negative impact upon Algiers.[1]

Algiers was a community of hard-working, God-fearing people and after it, it stopped. You can't put a thousand poor people who lost almost everything in the development without offering any service and not even spiritual upliftment

1. For a decent overview of Urban Renewal programs in New Orleans, see, Kent B Germany, *New Orleans After the Promises: Poverty, Citizenship, and the Search for the Great Society* (Atlanta: University of Georgia Press, 2007).

which I believe is the key, after any disaster, I think that's the foundation for recovery. It had an impact on all of us at St. Stevens.

Meeting Robert King in Algiers

Well, I knew his mother and his sister. I also know a lot of the King family because they all came up in the same church.

At one time it was across the street where Fischer Community Church is. That's where it was. That's the original and then they moved to the new location. The bigger church that they built there on the opposite side.

His [the Pastor's] name was Arthur Monday. He fought for residents' rights and that's the reason why that church is still there located where it's at, but now it's Fischer and at that time it was St. Stephen's until they bought the property across the street.

Yeah, 'cause King's sister was a staple in that church. Verna Mae was the one who greeted you when you first came in. You saw her for at least about thirty, maybe thirty or forty years and then all the while her kids is coming out. 'Cause that's what she would do. She was an Usher. That was part of my family, the church too. My brother and my sister belongs to there, but my brother is one of the ministers at St Stephens when he come into town.

I was living on Hendee and King was living on Sumner at that time, and I don't know if that's where they was living when King came home. That's where I met King's family.

They was a God-fearing, hardworking people. They just happened to be poor. Most of us, we came up in the time that most of the houses in Algiers had outdoor plumbing so like many of us, they had an outhouse.

I'd say King was about—because he's six years older than me—so I was about ten or eleven. He was about seventeen, I think. Yeah, he was much older than me. He had me for six years. I know I didn't see him during my teen years so it was during the time I was in elementary school so I had to be about ten, between 5th and 6th grade.

He was just a little Black youth coming out of reform school. I know that he had tried his hand at boxing 'cause his brother was a boxer. We had a lot of boxers coming out of Algiers and he used to sing. He had a little band that he used to sing with. In Algiers he was known as a stand-up guy... but I can't recall because, again, it was a six-year gap in between us so I didn't really know King, I knew of his family.

New Orleans Parish Prison

I really knew King when he started escaping from out the Parish Prison. We have a kinship of being from over here in Algiers. You get to learn about people simply because he was an Algerian—and the next time I heard about King was when he was in the Parish Prison because he was known as an escape artist. He knew how to get out of jail.

We was on C-1. I believe King was on C-3 and all of a sudden one night it started raining and they coming out of the wet. They had done an escape and King was one of the ringleaders of that escape and that's where I first [saw him]. That's one of the things him and Albert had in common. Albert escaped out of the courthouse. King escaped out of Parish Prison.

He said after he had gotten thirty-five years for a crime he didn't commit, ya dig? Shiiiit. He did just like most people. He's got to do one thing: either accept it or he can fight it and he's one of the ones who choose to fight it in the only way that he could use as a Black, poor Black man in New Orleans 'cuz he escaped at a time when they had check-ins. It was just like during slavery, either you accept being a slave or you reject it and King was one of the ones that rejected it.

I did all my time on death row or down on C-1. When we got arrested, they had put us on death row and that was on the 5th tier and then when it was too many of us to keep on the 5th tier, they put us on what at that time was the dungeon. That was C-1, and they had C-2, C-3, C-4 and then C-5, on the 5th floor, that was death row at one time or the dungeon, but it was the dungeon when we got arrested and then they put everybody out of there. They made C-1 the dungeon and C-1 at one time was just a closed tier 'cuz they had that messed up.

I didn't have, really very little. Except King and I, when he was on—what was they called it?—It was one of 'em police station that he was in. Yeah. That's when I found out that King was dealing with the Party and it is always that thing that you always love to hear about a homeboy, you dig, that's getting involved in the struggle that you are in.

So that's the first time I heard mention of King as it related to the Black Panther Party. Shelly Batiste, another giant. Ronald Ailsworth, he was there. All of them was over there in the First Precinct together.

They move King there after they caught him. They're some real standup guys over there at First Precinct and King was one of them. The jail sit on top of the police station so you ain't jumping out of no window there and escape [laugh] because you got the police, all these police right under you, ya dig, but they stood strong. All of the guys that went over there the First and couldn't too many people do what they did, very few people could do what they did.

They stood up in some of the toughest forms of incarceration. Shit, in Angola where they send people to Closed Cell Restricted as punishment, King and them thrived there, and the First—they'll send you from the Parish Prison to the First as punishment. King and them thrived in there, so again, some of the hardest times they went through it.

Angola

A lot of people think I was in Angola. I ain't never been to Angola. Most of the time I was at Angola, there, at first with Sister Helen Prejean. Well at one time, I was working with a group called Pilgrimage for Life. It was an abolitionist group and we did a march right after they brought back the death penalty, ya dig? That was for Wayne Williams, who was the first person to get executed when they brought back the death penalty and we did a march the day of his execution from Angola to Baton Rouge. So, on that walk, that's when I found out that CCR and Death Row was combined you dig? I mean it was all in the same area. That's when I also found out that King had become a well-renowned jailhouse lawyer writing writs and shit.

I know King has helped a whole lot of people that was on Death Row write their writs. If I'm not mistaken, he helped Albert write his, ya dig and I know this dude, Gary Tyler. He helped him. Thomas, John Thomas. He helped him write their writs. He really helped a whole lot of people.

At one time, if you even mentioned them in Angola you went to the hole, if you mentioned their name. Shit as soon as you mention their name you went to the hole. A guy now who is well-known for doing time in there and he's out and he was speaking at an engagement. This was during the time when we was doing Pilgrimage for Life and I just mentioned their name. I didn't mention King. I mentioned Albert and Herman. Shit and he went off on me, "Man, you trying to get me locked up! I've seen how it was and I've seen how effective [it was] . . . prisoners would rather fuck over each other than to stand together . . . and I've seen the impact all the time on the streets.

The jailhouse mentality is the common mentality out here and they need to know the brothers that stood up to this shit and that this don't break everybody. It only broke the fucking weak. The code that we was raised on that it was too tough for everybody else, it's just right for us. That's how my brother taught me and that's always been a thing and

I've always said, get rid of the weak and the suckers and see what you've got left.

And with us, I would say 90% of us we ain't going to do nothing. We might sit around and talk bullshit to each other. But we ain't going to challenge nothing. The whole Civil Rights Movement was probably 3 percent of African American population who participated in that and half of that participated in the Black Power. But I can't tell you how many motherfuckers I know that come up to me and tell me that their daddy and their mamma or their brother was in the Party and fuck I was the OG. I knew who everybody is. Shit, I ain't never heard of 'em, but I don't say nothing because I don't want to embarrass 'cause your Pa said this and that about how he was a Panther, but there was very few of us willing to make those kinds of stands. That made it easier for me to accept myself for sure 'cause if I had to do it all over again, I wouldn't do it.

Fuck no. I would never take my family through the hardships that I took them through by supporting anything and being where we were out here, being a member of the Black Panther Party in Louisiana anything we did . . . if I had to do it all over again, nah . . . poor Black man and I've seen it all. I'm 74 years old and I still got ten years of my health.

Visiting Angola

The first time that I ever met King as a man, we had went there for a visit. That was the only time that I got to visit at

Angola. Burl Cain never let me forget that either because see, I went there as Malik Rahim and they had me blackballed as Donald Guyton. So there the stupid motherfuckers couldn't put the two together. I'm in there. That was the only time I saw all three of 'em. Marina Drummer was seeing Herman and Leslie was meeting Albert, ya dig, and I went there with 'em and I guess I was pulled to see King because I knew all three of 'em was there at the same time and that was the one visit that I had while they was incarcerated. The next time I seeing King, that was after he was out.[2]

Angola 3

I found out about them from Colonel Boldt. I believe he did 17 years in solitary and when he got out, he's the one who told me Albert was going to trial. Geronimo had just got out. We was at an event that we was giving for Geronimo at Mission High School [in San Francisco] and Colonel Boldt came up asking for me, but under Donald Guyton. At first, I wasn't going to tell him and I said, "Yeah bro, what's up?" He said, "Man I just left one of your former partners." I said "who?" He told me "Albert Woodfox." He said "Albert had been granted another trial" and so then we started the

---

2. Burl Cain was the Warden at Angola, and now serves as the commissioner of the Louisiana Board of Corrections. Marina Drummer was a cofounder of the International Committee for Free the Angola 3.

Support Committee for 'em, but it was for the Angola 2. No one could've told me then but by the time G [Geronimo] got out that King was still being incarcerated.[3]

When we found out that Albert was going to trial, Richard Becker—he had organized the speaking engagement for Geronimo. Geronimo had just got out the day before ya dig and Richard gave that one—well, they gave one in L.A. and Richard gave the one up in San Francisco at Mission High School. When we found out that Albert was going to trial, I didn't even have to tell Richard, about it at that time, the Angola 4 ya dig, 'cause he had already know and he had done articles on the Angola 4 so he knew about that trial. I didn't have tell him. He gave us office space let us use his computers. And then when we went to New York for that Workers World Conference, they gave me a chance to speak to everybody that was there that was part of Workers World and pass that information out about Angola 3. I met Marina because I was told to watch over her 'cause Marina was a flaky white girl and I don't want to see nothing happen to her, ya dig, and then while we at the airport she lose her glasses, ya dig, so just sitting next to her, ya dig, we developed a conversation about the Angola 3, ya dig, by the time we got to Jordan, we had all these flyers that we passed out to everyone and there we met activists from all over the world.

3. Panther Geronimo Ji-Jaga Pratt served twenty-seven years in prison for a murder that FBI's own surveillance files showed that he was hundreds of miles away from. Jack Olsen, *Last Man Standing: The Tragedy and Triumph of Geronimo Pratt* (New York: Knopf, 2001).

Sometimes I feel guilty about getting Marina involved. Nobody gave her credit for it and shit something she ain't got to do. Marina is a white woman just like you, ya dig. The last thing that she had to do was worry about some motherfucking Black inmates in Louisiana but she stood up for it from the time I told her and that was on the road to Baghdad. We was going to Baghdad at the start of the war, which is the reason why right now I can't travel overseas. They took my passport. That's where I met Marina and Marina played a major role in taking it to that next level.

1998 Trial

When Albert was going to trial, we used to go all the way up to Amite to the court but then we had to leave and leave early enough that we'd be on the highway back to New Orleans before it get dark. Because we know that we in the heart of—excuse my expression—Crackerville and I know in that area those motherfuckers hated us and they hated y'all more than they hate me cuz they figured that y'all was traitors to the race y'all supporting these niggers. "What the fuck are y'all doing here with this bullshit talking about free the Angola 3?" I've seen the hatred that they had not basically but for me, I've seen that hatred for Ann and Bryce—I watched that hatred—and for Luis Talamantez. I watched the hatred that they pulled. Same day that Albert was found guilty.

Shit. I know, ain't no fucking way that Albert was gonna win that trial. The lawyers was selling him out. Ya dig and we get up in there and have a section of all of the supporters of him, and we probably took up about 20% of the courtroom. The rest was nothing but police from that area all in uniform. There ain't no fucking way he going to beat this here.

I said "Man there ain't no way in the world they going to win and Albert's going to walk out of here." Everybody talking about that and the lawyers telling 'em "Y'all shouldn't even be here. Y'all should be getting ready to give a party for him." But anyway, I knew he could never even stand a snowball chance in hell. It had a better chance of walking out of hell than Albert had walking out of that courtroom. I've seen that in the day. I watched that and I guess the most amazing part is like I told you was Marina, ya dig, Ann, Dick Becker and Gloria La Riva—they was with Workers World, now they have an organization called ANSWER.

I know they would still be unknown if it wasn't for people like y'all who stand for justice. It's really easy for me and him to get involved because we are constantly getting kicked in our ass. Y'all aren't getting kicked in y'all ass, ya dig. Y'all have no reason to get involved in the struggle other than because of justice. You can't say that I'm working for justice but I can say that you are because you are doing this interview. I'm going to tell you that the interview might be well accepted around the world, but it ain't going to be accepted here. It will not be accepted here.

Leslie and Marina came to visit them. That was the first time that ever happened. First time a billionaire went to Angola in the Angola history was to visit Albert ya dig? And that's when the warden pulled her out of you know out of the visiting room and said, "Shit what the fuck do you know what you are doing? These motherfuckers hate white folks. And you're visiting them. Don't go for that naive bullshit." And that's when Anita went off on them, ya dig, and got him straight. "You guys are talking to the wrong person. I'm not a naive white woman from Europe." Ya dig? "I know when there's an injustice." She got home. She went home in such a rage that she was sitting there, from what I was told, having breakfast with her husband and had a heart attack and died. That's what made Gordon Roddick get involved in the plight of the Angola 3, ya dig, and his daughter.

People That Don't Get Recognition

Opal Joiner. I know you've never even heard of her. Opal made a sacrifice for him, ya dig, been saying this for—there's a whole lot of motherfuckers now come out the closet about how they supported King and how they supported the Angola 3 and they ain't did a fucking thing when the heat was on.

When it became well known, that's when a lot of them came, especially after Anita Roddick got involved. That's when a lot of 'em came. But before then I remember a whole bunch of 'em, they ain't wanted to hear nothing about no Angola 3 'cause one of the things that even organizations that uh, what's that Jericho Movement up in Oakland? Even they didn't want to get into it. Some others said they wasn't no political prisoners and it wasn't until

Geronimo got out that the Angola 3 became accepted as political prisoners. Before then shit I had arguments and damn near had to fight motherfuckers behind that, ya dig, they saying that these guys wasn't worthy to be called political prisoners.

I said "Well fuck, if King is not, if they not political prisoners than George Jackson is not one, ya dig, 'cause who's political about a $70 gas station robbery, ya dig, so if you saying that . . ." You know, that's one of the things that we had a big argument about. As soon as I said that a lot of 'em fired up . . . 'cause one thing about it see if you are not an Albert Woodfox or King the average motherfuckers that was in this movement, they don't get shit. They don't have nothing. Most of them are doing bad.

Angola 3 in Perspective

You got to remember prison isn't nothing but an extension of slavery. You might call 'em a convict or an inmate, but really, they ain't nothing but a slave. When people come to that awareness that I'm not kept here because of a crime I committed, I'm kept here because I'm looked upon as a threat. As a Black man that comes from an oppressed community that is a threat to the white establishment, ya dig, that's totally against you—especially in the South.

You see a lot of 'em they turn political and that's what made King and 'em so dangerous because none of them was in there for no political charge: King, Albert, or Herman, but they turned political and that was a virus or a cancer that they didn't want spread throughout the prison. That's why Angola went from being one of the most notorious prisons to one of the most really docile and Christian communities, ya dig, 'cause many other prisons where you talk about that many prisoners that's doing life or practical life and . . . you start seeing generations 'cause with King and them was, you know, again, they was exceptional.

You know, I'ma tell you. They knew King wasn't in Angola [and] couldn't have been involved in that murder 'cause how can you kill somebody in Angola and be in Parish prison at the same time? That's just impossible. The main thing that they were all charged with, they had too much influence. They had too much influence on the prison. I don't believe that even the Warden at that time, Henderson, I believe, was his name believed that King and 'em killed the guard. But they believed that through their influence they took, which would normally be, prisoners that only fuck over each other. To do something like this, that was the first time a guard was killed in Angola. So, you know, basically, they locked King and 'em up and they made sure that'll never happened again and they throw them in, like I said, CCR was a disciplinary camp that's where they sent ya at to break you. I'd say usually, the average inmate might last a month, two months in CCR and then they're being broken but if they don't break 'em there they send them to Camp J and if Camp J didn't break you, ya dig? I would say maybe 90% of the ones that was in Camp J was broken either mentally, spiritually, you dig, especially politically. It took all that out of you there, and in these places, they thrive, ya dig, so, you know, it take a hell of a motherfucker to go through that, ya dig? Shit, I mean to be locked down like that.

King and them had to go before a hearing every six months and that's all they had to say is: "I renounce that Black Panther bullshit." I'm saying it in a negative way 'cause if they would have say it like that, they would have been out of CCR and for them to stay in there and endure what they did for—especially King for twenty-nine years, ya dig, when they tried to tried hook King up with everything from a murder while he was down there.

Even though I believe everybody on the tier said that King didn't kill the dude. They still charged King with murder, ya dig, so from that to what they was doing up in there and it was, it would take a hell of a person to endure this for twenty-nine years. But they did not know, they was trying to find something to keep him. They were trying to find something to keep him incarcerated and so they figured that eventually he was gonna beat that and come out of CCR behind the Brent Miller case, so then they put a murder to keep him so they kept him there for twenty-nine years and that was personal at that time right there and King did every day of it until he got out.

King's release

After King got out—I wasn't there when he got out because at that time, I was basically breaking away from the Angola

3 Support Committee. I was still speaking on their behalf. I was speaking about them, but I was no longer a part of the Angola 3 Support Committee. When King got out, my oldest son's daughter, she had lost one of her legs so I was in L.A. with her when King got out. I wasn't there. I saw King maybe about a month and a half after he had gotten out.

That was here [in New Orleans]. Him and a sister that was [long pause] that I owe so much to, Marion. Marion and King was together and that's when I really start hooking up with him. And so, after that, going to prison, a lot of prison events about Albert and Herman, ya dig, King and I would ride together and so we got, you know, we used to talk about it then and listening to him sing, ya dig and I don't know how he do it now, but at that time, Sam Cooke.

Oh man that's what I'm saying it's been some fucking years. [Laughs] Oh, yeah. That was King's thing. Yeah. That was his thing was Sam Cooke. That was his man there. I couldn't tell you 'cause when I saw King, it was maybe about a month later but he was still making the adjustment of being out on the street, but that's any inmate. Ron had to do forty years. My brother-in-law did fifty years and he's making that adjustment so you just can't do that kind of time, and especially the kind of time that they did, without seeing a different impact.

That's when King had moved to Austin. I was riding with him, going to his house for a number of hours and he told me on the highway that day that "I used to remember being in my cell thinking about this." Certain things have, certain statements coming from a person's experience have a profound effect upon me. I can't say this about everybody. It had a profound effect upon me cuz I could remember when I was locked down sometimes, I used to believe, not that I was driving, but doing other things.

Remembering other places and things like this. I couldn't imagine because I only did eleven months in solitary so and I couldn't imagine doing twenty-nine years of solitary like he did. In Herman and Albert's case over forty years in solitary I mean, it's hard to fathom. It's hard to fathom that I would take another human being and treat him that way. But they was used as an example. It was an example that worked because it turned Angola into a religious institution. You got more religious groups at Angola than anywhere, any other prison than I know of, and they using it now at all the other satellite prisons. That is because either you get into that bible or they's gonna lock your ass up.

I guess the biggest thing that I like to hear King when he say it, he used to say "Angola might be free of me but I ain't through with Angola," ya dig, and he stayed that way until he helped get his other two comrades out.

About Jessica Gingrich

Jessica Gingrich is a freelance writer, researcher, and podcast producer. Her writing has appeared in Gastro Obscura, Narratively, *and* Smithsonian Magazine, *among other publications. She cohosts and produces* FORKLORE *on HRN, produces the* Many Roads to Here *podcast, and contributes to the* Lost

Women of Science *podcast. Her audio stories have also been featured on KCRW's* Good Food *podcast, as well as on HRN's* Meat and Three *and* Amuse News. *In addition, Jessica is the Outreach Coordinator for BC Voices, where she plays a key role in amplifying women's history and advocating for social justice through storytelling.*

Common Ground organizers, Robert Hillary King, Lisa Fithian, Malik Rahim and scott crow. Credit: Ann Harkness /eMERGENCY heARTS.

Finding Common Ground
Interview with James R. Tracy

Common Ground Relief was one of two major black-led grassroots responses to Hurricane Katrina in 2005. Federal and local efforts worked as intended—systematically victimizing Black, Brown, and poor communities by providing punishment where relief was needed. Malik Rahim, working initially with a small group of seasoned activists founded Common Ground. Attracting hundreds of thousands of (mostly) young people to go south to do the work that the state was unwilling and unable to do. The collective helped residents salvage belongings, opened health clinics, fed displaced people, and worked to publicize conditions in New Orleans to a national audience.

Echoing the COINTELPRO repression of the Black Panther Party, it was revealed later that one of Common Ground's cofounders, Brandon Darby, had worked as an informant for the Federal Bureau of Investigation on multiple occasions. The mistrust sewn by Darby, created deep divisions within the collective? Despite this, Common Ground remains an example of effective mutual aid as is increasingly studied as a model for humanitarian relief in an era of climate chaos.

The Days Before the Storm

At first, Katrina went from Florida. Everybody thought that Katrina had missed us. Then it turned around and came back. It happened at the worst time of the year to be poor in Louisiana, especially in New Orleans. It happened right after school started. Everybody that was poor was really broke because they had spent everything on getting their kids in school and getting their school supplies and uniforms and things like this, and it was all just about waiting for the first. *I might have enough dough to last me until the first. I'm going to make it to the first. That's the mindset that we still had.*

We knew that there was 160,000 poor people that didn't have no way of evacuating. This is a city of just under 500,000. At least the fourth of them didn't have no way of getting out of here. So, when Katrina turned back around and started heading toward here and Mayor Ray Nagin gave the evacuation order, that was when Katrina hit that Sunday. When he gave the evacuation order and you start seeing everybody packing to leave, that's when you start seeing the difference, not only between Black and white but between rich and poor.

Everybody who had money left, and the poor that was here was stuck. A bunch of us who live in Algiers, we all met at a partner of mine's backyard, Henry "Pal" Alexander. He was the President of the Westbank Steppers, our Second Line in Algiers. That's where we all hung out. If you have been to prison, especially if you have been to prison, and you get out, you going to come by his yard. It's just the spot. We met the day before the hurricane hit. We decided on who going to leave and who going to stay. We were all making plans. Algiers is a community that in my seventy-four years has never flooded. We all thought it was going to be cool. I was a drywall contractor, and I had all my tools put up in my attic. We were making plans for how we were going to help each other out after the storm. *You come on over afterwards. You do my roof. I do your drywall*. We were making those type of plans, those who did construction. Before Katrina, 80% of the construction in city of New Orleans was done by African Americans. There was a bunch of African Americans that I knew who used to do that work.

We sat up. We talked about the neighborhoods. I was able to talk to some brothers, who I didn't know if they were going to stay. I urged them to check in on their neighborhoods. *Find out how elders were staying. How many kids going to be here? We can start looking out for each other now*. As Katrina started getting closer, I saw some of the worst in people. I don't how to describe it. I've seen people who knew that everything in the refrigerator and their freezer was going to go bad, but before they would give it to anybody, they said, *Fuck, I'd rather let this shit stay in my refrigerator and go bad. I ain't getting it to nobody*. Neighbors who had two and three cars, they couldn't leave town with all of them. They would rather let a car get flooded than to loan it to another. That was the traumatic part for me of the day before Katrina hit. Then there were so-called community leaders pack up and leave. The time your community needs you most. You're gone.

When it was safe for them to return, the politicians and so-called leaders, they come back and want to talk about, *This is the community I represent*. That *was* the community, why wasn't you there? I can understand you getting your folks out of harms away, but you are supposed to be a community leader, and you're saying that you represent this community. Then you should have come back and made sure that your community was safe. That was the traumatic part, and the reason why I said traumatic, is because it still leaves a profound impact upon me to, even talk about it, even try to remember those days when I saw the worst side of people in this city.

I've been organizing my entire life, but this time I was just preparing for survival. Because I didn't think it was going to be as bad as it was. I thought we were going to probably go through with the norm, go a week without power. Then after that, power was back on and you to start doing, making a little money and stuff. I was just preparing to survive. When it hit, the lady I was with at the time was Sharon Johnson, she stuck with me during the most difficult moments of Katrina.

If Katrina would've happened after the fifteenth of September, I would've been in San Francisco. I had been planning on moving back to there. I had already talked with Reverend Jeff Branner and others. I was just wrapping with my mother's affairs and had to do a few more things to help my family here. I wanted to be there in time for the anniversary celebrations in Oakland of the founding of the Black Panther Party for Self Defense. The last thing I wanted to do at this point in my life was organize again.

Welcome to the Terrordome

Then when hurricane came, we kept hearing this [makes whooshing sound] in the wind. A hurricane moves counterclockwise, and by the fact that it go counterclockwise, we were able to tell the time it would hit land by the rotation of that hurricane. When the rotation started getting quicker, and you know it's about to hit. You feel this breeze here and suddenly it will pass, then it might be twenty minutes or an hour, and you feel that breeze again. You know it is coming.

By the time it got close, that's when they officials started saying that maybe about 60,000 people were going to lose their homes, by the time it was over, and that's when it got desperate. I never seen a city in such a panic state. Then right before Katrina happened, I would say the last, at least the last twelve hours. That's when they finally opened up the Superdome. They must have had about six, eight different police departments in this area just at the Superdome. It had two or three different National Guards at the Superdome. They searched everybody in the rain before they let them in. They was searching them for alcohol, or drugs, weapons. The police searched everybody before they let them in the Superdome. That's why when that bullshit in the media came out all the horrors of the Superdome, we knew it was fake. It felt like the state was spoiling for a fight.

After the hurricane hit, things were very calm over the river here in Algiers. I cleaned up my yard then, and I was all cutting my grass. Because the street just about the way it is here. You couldn't really tell there had been a hurricane from over here. I cut my grass, and that's when my brother told me about the flood across the road. I had one of the few landlines that was up and running. "Man, where are you?" he said sounding panicked. I told him that I was at home cutting my grass. "New Orleans is flooding!" He yelled through the telephone line.

The last person I spoke to before the flood was Robert King. I told him to come and ride out the storm over here. We went back and forth. He decided to ride it out at his house. I decided to ride it out here. But Sharon Johnson and I had just really started back talking again about a week or something before the hurricane. I was telling her about moving back to California. We always had that respect for each other. Right before the hurricane, I called her to ask her, what was she was going to do. And she said that she was going to stay at her house. I told her, I said, "Listen, where you at has this problem of flooding, don't get caught there." That's when she phoned me to tell me she was going to the Superdome. "You're going to Superdome? Don't tell me you're going to the fucking Superdome." She did.

I had some friends go in and get them and bring her to my house. They ran and got her brought back here with another guy. We rode out the hurricane together. As that wind was blowing, when it come around, it could lift the house. You feel it settling back down, lifting up, settling back down. That's when I decided, I'll never ride out another one. That if it come, I'm going to be away from it, be at least a hundred miles away from that motherfucker. I never ride out another hurricane. After that, we started going over and help with the rescue.

The Other Battle of Algiers

When we met in Algiers, it was about thirty of us. Twenty-nine were formerly incarcerated persons. Only one person had never been to prison, and he had the street moniker of Killer, everybody else had been to prison. Because most of the people that stayed were formerly incarcerated and again, the reason why they stayed is because of the fact that they had a family now, that couldn't leave. They had a wife or a girlfriend or children, and children's mother, didn't have a car, and didn't want to leave, or didn't want to leave in a stolen car.

This happened at a time that most people was broke, and that was a lot of reason why a lot of people wouldn't leave and go away. The city ain't had no fucking plan. The only plan was the Superdome and that didn't open until 12 hours before the hurricane hit. It didn't, so if a person didn't have nothing, *Where I'm going? How I'm going to get there*? What I'm going to do when I get there? Then shit, I rather ride it out here. At least I'm home.

They think everybody knew that the [public housing] projects was the safest place because then the projects were made of brick. It was understood stood every hurricane from Betsy until Katrina. So, everybody knew well, *Hey man, listen, we're going to all go in the projects and ride it out there, and that was the thing, and that's what we're going to do.* We're going to ride out the hurricane at a housing project. That's where we're going to ride it out. People didn't have nothing. You were only able to bring what you could fit on your lap to the Superdome. You couldn't bring nothing else. I don't believe they even let you bring water or food. Again, a lot of people went to the Superdome. Sharon stayed over here with me, and that was a blessing for both of us.

The guys wouldn't let me get in the water. They tell me, *Listen, you stay on the freeway. We'll bring people to you.* I saw them take tires off cars and use that as floating devices, saw them take refrigerators and tear the door off to throw off and pull the mortar out of it and use that as a floating device. Individuals took their boats out looking for people to rescue. At first, these rescues were done at first with the police. All of a sudden, I seen police go from supporting the community rescuers to arresting people.

No Exits

It's easier to kill a nigger than to kill a Black man. Demonization is the first thing they want to do. Then, all you hear all about the looting. None of that happened until people realized that *I'm on my own. I ain't got nothing. Nobody's providing anything. I'm on my fucking own.* I've never seen that the way I saw it after Katrina.

When people realized that *Hey, man, we got to get out of here. Because the fucking levee going to break over here. I got to get out.* All the busses were flooded across the river because they didn't use them. So that's when they went into the bus garage here and started taking the buses, which is the most, that's the part that really made me feel good. Because people started taking the buses and parking it in front of the housing projects. *Hey, man, tomorrow morning, we're gone. So come on, get on the bus.* They loaded people up on the bus, getting them out on time. That's the part that really got me, seeing how they was evacuating. They go over here without any governmental assistance they found, the buses, and found the people. Those buses went all around the country. Getting people where the needed to go, family, friends, shelters.

The driver would tell them, "We're going to Atlanta. If you want to come on, get on this bus. We're going to Houston." You dig? You saw them buses pulling off and people going away. That happened like that on Tuesday and Wednesday, but Wednesday evening, everything changed. On Wednesday evening, it went from you were able to cross the bridge to a total lockdown. If you were Black, you were locked down. If you were Black, you couldn't walk in certain areas. White vigilantes started to posse up feeling emboldened. My first confrontation with one of them, my neighbor, was that Thursday. One of my Black neighbors came around the corner, all shook up, and said, "Motherfucker, those boys tried to kill me. They're around the corner, and they pulled guns on me and told me to run, and I know if I would've ran, they was going to shoot me down." I didn't believe it. "I said, Man, come on. Let's go around and see what's going on."

I knew one of the men, he stayed around there on the next street. I went to him. I said, "Man, what's going on?" Then I've seen a couple of that I didn't recognize, and one of said, "You don't owe that nigger no explanation." I could see that this wasn't going to end well. If it wasn't for this elderly white woman, who used to stay on the block on that side of the street. She came out on the porch, and I believe that stopped them from killing both of us. I told him, "You ain't coming on this motherfucking block here. You ain't coming here with that bullshit. Not on this street here."

They saw Sharon at the door, but they couldn't tell whether she was a man or a woman, and they saw my neighbor there and other brother that was with me, that was standing right on the side of the house. They didn't know how many of us it was. But I know in that truck that they had, they had a driver and a passenger in the front seat, and they had two in the back of the truck, standing up with rifles, and both on the front seat, they had on the dashboard, two pistols. I saw how well armed it was and how much ammunition they had. I saw that they had cases of ammunition. But by the fact that they didn't know how many of us here, they just pulled off.

Right after that, the same guys broke into the local pawnshop. In the back of the pawnshop, they had a trailer that was damn near full of guns. They took all the guns out of the pawnshop, but then there was guns without no ammunition. I thought, "These motherfuckers ain't nothing but clubs." You can't do nothing with it. You ain't got no bullets for these different weapons.

If you were Black, you couldn't go over the bridge right here. If you were Black and from New Orleans, if you didn't have Jefferson Parish identification, you couldn't go into Jefferson Parish. Quarantined, that's it. Whites was able to go back and forth as they pleased. If you was Black, you was quarantined. Everybody talked about how they treated. You can't try to cross the bridge coming over here, because the evacuation station was the ferry in Algiers. You had to walk across the bridge and then after the hurricane, the temperature was like about 96°, 97°, with the heat index making it around 105°, 100% humidity. You dig? It wasn't on the hot and humid, but it was stuffy. When you start seeing people coming over here, exhausted. A lot of them didn't have no water.

And they couldn't go through Algiers Park to get there. They had to walk on the ledges of the levees. The cold part about it, the water here was never turned off in Algiers. This was the only place that had fresh drinkable water after the hurricane because people, listen, from Pascagoula, Mississippi, all the way to Morgan City was coming here to this water treatment plant right down the street to get water.

There was no way that Blacks would be allowed to enter Gretna and further south. Gretna didn't flood so nobody had to leave the area to other parts of the nation. Algiers didn't flood, Gretna didn't flood. Harvey didn't flood. Westwego didn't flood. We had enough places here. Nobody had to be evacuated out of state. They wanted to take the city back. They knew that there were thousands that couldn't leave, that was stuck in the city. Well, 99% of them were Black. They shot them out of the state. Nobody had to leave New Orleans. I'm sitting up here and I'm watching this. I'm watching the governor give a shoot to kill curfew. That only applied to Blacks.

A white person could come through there at any time. And I'm telling you that because when we founded Common Ground, that's what they were able to do when I couldn't leave this porch after dark. They were able to use their white privilege to go and get supplies and bring them back here.

Two brothers told me, "Listen man this these motherfuckers shooting us trying to get to the ferry." The Algiers ferry was the evacuation station. The anger was so high, that one said, "I'll tell you what, if they're gonna shoot us, then we're not letting any white motherfucker get on this bridge. They have to come through us to get on the bridge. They're going to shoot at us we're going to shoot at them." I told him, that if a race war broke out, they were going to lose. We were not prepared to do nothing. You fail to plan, you plan to fail.

When we passed by the Fire Department, I was looking at cases of water from the floor to the ceiling. They wouldn't give out none of it. That's when one of the firemen told me said, "Listen, I shouldn't be telling you this, but I know you, you're my neighbor. Let people know that the water is off limits." I said, "Why are you telling this to me? You'll should be out there telling it to people when after you had them to walk across that fucking bridge, to come over here, to go to evacuation station."

If a hurricane happened right now, this season, we'll wind up going through the same thing. It might not be as bad as in 2005 with Bush, because Trump is out of the White House. I hope that Biden would not allow them to deny access to American citizens simply because they're Black. That happened during Katrina. It wasn't no equality after Katrina. The powers-that-be here said that this was a chance for them to seize New Orleans back. They believed that Katrina could do what the government had failed to do—get the Blacks out. We had a Black Chief of Police, Eddy Compass, and a Black Mayor, Ray Nagin. But it didn't matter. I thought, *How the fuck are you going to allow vigilantes to run up in your city?*

They were doing the business of the racists.

Nothing prepared me to those weeks, nothing. Being on death row, being in the dungeon, being in prison, nothing. Being in knife fights, being in gunfights, nothing prepared me to what happened in those two weeks. Nothing. I couldn't even remember all the lights out, and every now and then you hear gunshots going off. By the fact that we right across the river from the 9th Ward, as 8th ward flooded.

You could hear people with cans and stuff, hitting. You could probably hear some of them howling for help. I'd always walk on the levees and look at the water, that's my war room. That's where I go to get close to my ancestors. Go up there look around and then see what was going on. Nobody could have told me that in a city with a Black mayor, Black police chief, and Black congressman, that this kind of bullshit could go on. That's why I later ran for Congress as a member of the Green Party.

Over half of the police is Black at that time, now it's even more. You have this, you have a police captain that is Black, you have a sheriff that is Black, how the fuck this can be allowed to happen? How can you have vigilantes here and you come here and hurry up and suppress this. The killing of your people. A guy that was working for Blaine Kern who we call Mr. Mardi Gras. He told the police from up north, that they killed over thirty people. Over thirty people. Police asked him, "Well what you did with it? what you did with those bodies?" "Oh, we gave them to the Coast Guard." [That was where] Henry Glover body was cremated.[1]

Everybody said that the police set his body on fire after they killed him. Set his body on fire. They go back there and find out about death and look at what is right across the street from it. Here's the fire and right across the street is a US Customs headquarters. A guard on duty at the gate and here's a fire right across the levee and nobody from there even investigated.

See the mayor didn't have no power outside of Orleans Parish nor did the police chief. At the border, with Gretna, they had power in. But our congressman, he could have deputized some US Marshals and come down here, to Gretna,

---

1. Inci Sayki, "The Henry Glover Killing & the New Orleans Police Department's Efforts to End Federal Oversight," PBS Frontline October 24, 2023, https://www.pbs.org/wgbh/frontline/article/henry-glover-new-orleans-police-departments-consent-decree.

open up the fucking borders. But none of them did anything. They allowed the shit to play out.

Finally Got the News

I didn't know what to do. My friend Mary Ratcliff, coeditor of the *San Francisco Bay View* newspaper called me. My house still had a working landline, so she interviewed me about the conditions we were facing. She transcribed my call for solidarity and aid into an article, "This is Criminal." She sent that article to anyone who would read it. Amy Goodman of *Democracy Now!* soon arrived in town, as did AC Thompson, then a reporter for *The Nation*. I can't tell you enough how Mary Ratcliff helped our recovery efforts, she helped break the information blockade. So did AC, his early articles managed to expose the murder and corruption going on here.[2]

Many other people said that I was lying about what was in that *Bay View* article. *"That's Malik Rahim. You know he's a Black Panther? You know that's all he is a fucking hustler. He wants to do anything to start some bullshit."* I could go on and on. It didn't come out until later that everything I said was

---

2. Malik Rahim, "This is Criminal: Malik Rahim Reports from New Orleans," *San Francisco Bay View*, September 7, 2005, https://sfbayview.com/2008/11/this-is-criminal. A.C. Thompson's consistent reporting on Katrina lasted long after many news outlets abandoned the story. A.C. Thompson, "Katrina's Hidden Race War," *The Nation*, January 5th, 2009, https://www.thenation.com/article/archive/katrinas-hidden-race-war.

just true. The bridge murders happened. There were white vigilantes here. And that Gretna, just south of New Orleans, closed their borders to African Americans. Gretna still the most racist city in the nation. The majority of the police stops of a person in Jefferson Parish are Black men. Long before Katrina, they were going to stop Black men driving into Gretna. They don't care how many times, if he's young and Black, they're going to stop him. When they stop him, they're going to harass him in such a way that he will never want to come back into Gretna. That's the way it has always been there. In the aftermath of Katrina, they took their game up to a whole other level. And they are doing it still today, because of the fact that we were a city that refused to stand up to them. I get calls even today from some youngster telling me about what he just went through in Gretna. That even though the police said that they stopped him for this reason when he showed them his titles and insurance and all this and driver's license that they keep their boots on his neck and keep them on the ground and get two or three police cars on them.

Building Common Ground

It was about that time that activists scott crow and Brandon Darby arrived from Austin and showed up on my porch. I was probably an afterthought. They were here to rescue Robert King. They couldn't get across the river. They stopped here. That was on September 4th, right after the Danziger

Bridge shootings. scott came and said, "It's time that we do something. That we organize, because that was just blatant murder, that the police were able to get away with this."

I wasn't sure what to make of this, watching what's was going on. When Black people were arrested during this time, they weren't going to be released after just seventy-two hours. They were just held indefinitely, and the Governor's shoot-to-kill order loomed large. The community was scared, you would hear, *Man you know homeboy didn't make it back and the motherfucker was arrested, and he was killed.* This was unlike anything I've ever seen. I've seen people get killed. But I never saw bodies just laid out in the park, rotting. The heat made their bodies explode. Some of them had been half eaten by dogs, who had returned to their own wild state just to survive this disaster.

We had dead bodies in Algiers, that lay festering in this heat for about two weeks, and they wouldn't pick them up. We got three funeral homes in this area, so it didn't make any sense. They wouldn't allow the bodies to be picked up. We were talking about burying some of them. The cops said, *Nah you bury them, we're going to arrest you.* Later, we find out that the reason why was that a politician wanted to give a contract for body disposal to his supporters up in Texas. And he took them that long to get his act together. The air was just toxic. An odor unlike any odor I have ever experienced, and I've been tear gassed quite a few times.

I told scott about what was happening with the white vigilantes. Next time I see him, he came with a duffel bag full of weapons. I never forget that. Here's this guy, a white guy, coming here with weapons to protect me. That's when I started seeing his humanity. When scott said it's time for us to organize. I said, "What do you mean?" There is no way that we just stand up to this city, to this government like this. This was coming from me, a Black Panther. I told him that I won't be a part of nothing, that I got to be the main organizer for. If he was willing to take on that part, we could talk, because you couldn't pull anything off. Without some type of organized structure.

A few of us were sitting right here in my kitchen table, talking about social movements. How they always start off strong, with passion and purpose, and usually end in despair. That's what King said. "We have to find a common ground that everybody could stand on." That's how we landed on the name for what was to come. We founded Common Ground to help coordinate the grassroots relief effort coming in from all over the globe. We were applying the spirit of the Panther survival programs in new ways. Under that umbrella, we founded Common Ground Health Clinics, and Legal Services. I didn't expect to find myself back in the fray, but I was. We tried to organize ourselves in a way that if the state came down on one program, the others could survive. We were working together but separate at the same time. After that, scott left with King for Texas. They left Brandon Darby in New Orleans with me. That was like leaving Judas in the house with Christ.

Shortly after they left, I was walking up on the Algiers levee. This spring. That's where I meditate and pray, to find my spiritual self. I didn't think that we were going to be able to pull this off. When we founded Common Ground, I had $20, Sharon had $30. That was what we founded Common Ground with. I asked myself *What had I gotten myself into?*

People started coming to New Orleans from all over the country. I was sitting on the porch, and I saw a bus driving down the street, slowing down in front of my house. I went to the back and saw two big white guys approaching to the porch. I have my gun in my hand, and I was ready to shoot if they came up on my property. I mistakenly thought they were vigilantes. I said to myself, *these motherfuckers are coming up for some bullshit*. I am looking at their hands, and I wasn't going to let them go into their pockets to pull weapons.

"What are you looking for?" I yelled.

"We're looking for Malik Rahim. Are you Malik?" one guy yelled back. I figured *here we go again*.

"Yeah, I'm Malik."

"You can call me Bear, we are from Veterans for Peace."

When he said that my guard just went down because I have been to a Veterans for Peace event and worked with a local Veterans for Peace chapter. I know the good work they do. That's when they told me that they gathered all sorts of relief supplies for New Orleans and they wanted to drop it off with me. Bear said they didn't know what to do with the supplies, but knew I would. On the next day, another shipment of supplies came, then the following day, and more after that. Each time the shipment came, new people came as well. My next-door neighbor had left me his keys. We set in his house, as a computer lab. There was a computer room close to the backyard. In his yard and my yard, there were a bunch of tents.

I have seen some kids come down from Boulder, Colorado. They were going to the University of Colorado. They left, said they would pick up the supplies that Thursday. They loaded everything up on that truck and, Friday night, they drove those supplies down here. When they drove those supplies down here, as they unloaded them, they sit for maybe a couple of hours with us. Jump right back in the trucks and headed back to Colorado so that they could be in school for that Monday morning.

There came Street Medics. They came down with a goal, and immediately started saving lives. Roger was one of those medics and he started saving lives. Individuals came from Seattle, some of the same people who learned this kind of work Battle in Seattle, 1999.

Jimmy Dunson, one of the guys I still work with on mutual aid projects embodied the spirit that we previously saw in the antiglobalization movement. Don't wait for the government. The police took him to jail for double parking, right in front of the relief and distribution center. He was driving a big old Penske truck. Jimmy looked like he was about 12 years old behind that wheel. He was white, eighteen, and he was going into Fischer Projects, and all the projects in the area, on his own.

On his own. He would just find out what people needed, go get it and bring it back. One guy had a battery-powered wheelchair, after a while he had lost all power, so he couldn't use that, and had no way of charging his wheelchair. So that man, he was stuck. He told Jimmy that, the reason why he couldn't get around, about that wheelchair. The very next day, Jimmy took the wheelchair with him, to charge the wheelchair, and he brought him a manual wheelchair. That happened right out here. When I found out what he was doing, I went back then to the housing projects and I told the residents not to fuck with him or mess with him. They said *Don't mess with who?*

I said, *the white boy that be coming in that Penske truck.* They said *Who are you talking about? The Mac Man? Yeah, you're talking about Jimmy Mac!* They gave him that name and that's what they still call him. *Man, ain't nobody gonna mess with Jimmy back here* one of the residents told me. This was during the time of the shoot-to-kill curfew. It was the youngest volunteers at that time, between Katrina and Rita, that stopped New Orleans from going into a race war. Because of what they were doing.

Never in the history of the Woodland, that you've seen a white person walking through at no one o'clock in the morning. It wasn't heard of until we did it, and we ain't never had no incident. We never had no incident.[3]

Oh yes, indeed. I was buying two used tugboats and generators. For backup power on it. It can see the building was, the tallest building was five floors. So, with that antenna that we were putting up on. See, listen, we could cover the whole golf course, from right there to Woodland. We had people that

---

3. Jimmy Dunson, *Building Power While the Lights Are Out: Disasters, Mutual Aid, and Dual Power* (Tampa: Rebel Hearts Publishing, 2023).

were—registered everybody to vote. They gave everybody a job or you can't tell me about your late because you stay right here. So, you come into work. We was paying them all—what it was—$250 a week. $1,000 a month, and that's five hours. One hour every day had to go to civic responsibility. Where we going to work together, how we're gonna start this business. How we're going to start that business. Tell me about cooperative. We were in the process of sending a delegation to Spain. Spain has some of the best co-ops in the world.

Soon after that, two long black vans arrived, full of nothing but computers. That was the first time I saw the Guy Fawkes mask, aka Anonymous. It was just sitting on their dashboard. Yeah, I didn't know what it was at the time. I just looked at and I thought, they had, be down here, you going to a party. This is New Orleans, and masks is nothing like that seems out of the ordinary, to see a person with a mask. Most of the people in the van were wearing all-black. Their spokesperson told me "Just call me Blank." I thought *What the fuck is this*?

"What up man, how can I help you?"

"This is where the computer lab is?"

"Yeah. How can I help you?"

"Oh, man, we come here to help you all."

I said, "Well, come on then."

The anarchists set up an antenna the side of this house, part of setting up our own communications network. Sharon was scared to death of them. She was scared to go to sleep around them. I told her, "We got guns, we got a lock on the door. The fuck do we got to worry about?" and I got to get up and go to the bathroom. These guys proved their worth quickly. Blank and his crew set up an internet system that, that the city and the government couldn't break. A few days after that, I saw them under the bridge. When I say under the bridge, I don't mean on the ground of the bridge. I mean in way up in the catwalk! *What were they doing up the fuck up there?* You'll usually see people up there working. But I knew it was them because they dressed in black. When they walked down to the end when a ladder comes down. Then you got two floors, whereas not—you got to have something to get those two floors, so you go get to the bridge and they had their ladder. I said, look at these guys here. They were posting the relay equipment for our network just right there in the open. They had a firewall so great. I mean, had the computer so that, all you had to do is touch and it's popping up. This meant that Common Ground was able to have one of the first reliable livestreams during the crisis.

Shortly after that, Lisa Fithian arrived. She brought Starhawk and the rest of them. With them, we made a paradigm shift, from relief to environmental justice. We started making compost tea, spraying people's property because everything was toxic. Heavy metal is the reason why they call it heavy metal, it doesn't float. So, wherever the water gets discharged is just gonna settle.

Then we planted sunflowers, so that sunflower could pull the toxics out, break them down, the sunflowers are pulling poisons into the plant. Then we'll take the plant out in the bayou. Plant that, put that in the ground. We gonna let nature clean up this mess that we have made.

We started Common Ground on the 5th. By the 15th we probably had 200 people in and out of here. I'm telling you, all these areas, tents set up. Never had one sanitation problem. Set up our compost toilet. It was flooding, and the Superdome was full of filth, we ain't had none of that here.

Schools from around the country started sending their students here. We had students from a historically black college working to rehabilitate a school in the 9th Ward. This was about the time when a group of people from our health clinic and relief efforts were invited to visit. At that time, we had maybe, 2,000 or 3,000 volunteers.

The principal of the school said because this is a Black community, and this is a Black school, we're going to allow Black students to lead the struggle and come into the building and start doing the demolition. One evening, an official from one of the historically Black colleges came down and said "How dare you use our kids for a political thing?" As if we were exploiting kids.

Resistance and Repression

One day the police came here to find out what the fuck we were doing. They say that I had all these Black guys looting, and I'm selling it on the side of my house. So, they came that night to raid. It was the New Orleans police, the State police, and the National Guard. Now, the National Guard was a group out of California. The guy that was in charge was named Emmanuel Hernandez, he was the lieutenant colonel. When they came, if it would have been a porch full of Blacks, we would have probably all would have been jailed or killed. But when they came and there's just seeing them white kids. They took little Jimmy to jail for double parking.

There never would have been a Common Ground without this community coming together. I know, I couldn't have handled it alone, if it wasn't for what scott did. The next time I saw him, he came down with a trailer full of bicycles. Then suddenly, we start getting doctors coming in from all over—the Doctors without Borders. We started getting nurses from all over saying, *Hey, we've read that you trying to open up a health clinic. Here we are.* Within a month, we had started a health clinic. Natasha Dedrick, an activist from San Francisco, came down and brought a couple of doctors.

This is between the fifteenth and the nineteenth of September. On the nineteenth we opened up as a health clinic. There's no first aid station at the health clinic in four days. We had some Black doctors to try to come and help us. But even they couldn't get past Jefferson Parish. Jefferson turned them around. You dig? The clinic reminded me a lot of our Black Panther Serve the People programs, but different. It was started by a Jew and a Muslim. At the time, I was a practicing Muslim. He said how historic it was to think that the Muslim and the Jewish faith could come together.

First thing, after any kind of disaster, you must establish your spirituality. Every faith-based institution should have been made accessible for the relief efforts. That's why we took the effort to help faith-based get back established. That's the foundation, and then we used to—part of it we were teaching civic responsibility. That's been absent. People can look past just themselves, and we haven't learned from that. Because if we did, everybody that we helped would've helped somebody else, and New Orleans wouldn't have never—we won't even have to worry about if a hurricane comes, because we would be prepared because that civic component will still be here.

Infiltration

There were no problems between Lisa and Brandon and myself for a while. After that he started a slow campaign of divide-and-conquer. A meeting that normally would last a half an hour would drag on for two or three hours because of those two arguing. Constantly getting into it. That dragged on until I had to make a decision, which I sent Lisa to another parish. This is the parish that would never accept no aid from Blacks. They started their own relief organization called Hope. Because they didn't want to have any deals with me.

I asked Lisa, just to concentrate on the environmental program. Try to save this city. You all going to expose that these trailers, that they are giving people, are toxic. They helped me show them how they could deal with it. Because that's where the need was.

Brandon started to mess with the money. I'm going to show you how desperate he was. Bruce Springsteen came down, and he gave us a check for $200,000. Brandon conveniently loses the check then finds the check after it expired. This went against our practices. At first, any donation came strictly to Common Ground, and then have a collective decision on how to redistribute it among the projects. People wanted to give donations strictly for the clinic. I was telling that, no, you can't give strictly for the clinic. You'd donate to Common Ground. Then it comes to us, and we are going to collectively see how the fund will be distributed. That's the way it was.

We had a representative from the health clinic. Then a rumor started up, that I was taking money, opening a bank account in New Orleans, and shit like that. Whole kind of rumors starts. This was right after the People's Hurricane Relief Fund held its tribunal around the crimes of the U.S. government in the aftermath of the hurricane. I testified. The tribunal basically charged the government with genocide. Right after that, everybody was targeted. Every organization working for justice in New Orleans was targeted and lost their funding. It didn't hurt us as much at first, simply because we didn't have no paid staff. Every organization that had paid staff, wind up losing their funding, was dried up.

Then like I said, things had changed from just surveillance. Brandon, ceased to be the observer and became a provocateur. Brandon made a five-year commitment to work with me. That's what he told me, he said, man, I stand with you for five years. That's why it took me so long to face the facts. Motherfucker came down here to help me. That's why I couldn't go against him. I was down here with these motherfucking vigilantes, he and scott still found me.

Now people are going to tell me he's a police officer, and he trying to destroy this organization. Oh man, he was one of the founders. No, he ain't no police, man. He might be head strong. But he ain't no police. But even my son told me he thought he thought Brandon was the police, but I couldn't believe it. That Brandon was given the green light for the destruction of Common Ground.

I believe that Brandon wasn't always corrupt, he became corrupt. Austin, Texas was the home of Lisa and scott. The activists there were always under fire. There were so many fucking red flags. It wasn't a surprise that the FBI knew about us. Down here, everybody that came was a red flag to the FBI. Brandon's animal activism and other things that he was doing, had them on their list. You dig? Listen, when Lisa came. She helped put it together.

A lot of people ask if it was the trip to Iraq that attracted the government's attention. They weren't going to let something like Common Ground survive anyhow. When I got back, the federal government took my passport and driver's license. It was an easy way to sabotage me. I owned a truck back then. Motherfuckers come here and take the motor out and left. I've abandoned driving, because of the history of what they had in Common Ground, and I wasn't going to drive them. Because I wasn't gonna drive without a driver's license.

A Legacy Left

Never have a group of strangers, come together and provide services that we did, and a multitude of services. A person might say, well, *Did the Red Cross gave out more food?* Yeah, but what else did they do? Did they open a legal clinic or health clinic? Did they do home remediation? Did they tarp the roofs? Did they fix any houses? What else did they do besides the basics? What else did they do? Any other organization that you could name. None of them did the multitude of things that we did. Because they weren't providing anything. If we wouldn't have provided the service that we did, New Orleans would be nowhere near the way it is now, because of us. If all you do is nothing, and you all believe that there's no reason to doing anything, you have already lost. For most people didn't do anything. But, those who did, with true conscience of this nation, was ringing that bell. That's the decree on this Common Ground. It was those with conscience, that came together, as strangers. Only here for one common purpose, that common ground, that brought them here. To show what humanity is supposed to be.

About James R. Tracy

James R. Tracy is a long-time organizer and educator. He currently serves as the Chair of the Labor and Community Studies Department. He is the cofounder of the San Francisco Community Land Trust. Tracy is the coauthor of Hillbilly Nationalists, Urban Race Rebels and Black Power: Interracial Solidarity in 1960s-70s New Left *and* No Fascist USA! The John Brown Anti-Klan Committee and Lessons for Today's Movements. *He is the author of* Dispatches Against Displacement: Field Notes From San Francisco's Housing Wars. *He lives in Oakland, California.*

Malik Rahim talks strategy with Common Ground Relief volunteers.
Credit: Todd Sanchioni

Climate Justice and the Prisoners' Struggle Go Together

Interview with Mansa Musa

Mansa Musa: One thing I was looking at was your work on the environment, and what really got me looking at that was, that I remember me, Eddie, and Dominique, in North Carolina, we were having a conversation. Eddie said that he felt and believed that the direction that the young people would take in terms of organizing and mobilizing would be around the environment.

And when he said it, I was saying to myself, that really doesn't make sense. But as I thought about it, it does make a lot of sense because they're the ones it's going to hurt, the environment, and they're the ones that do a lot of interaction with the environment in terms of going out, boating, picnicking, or taking a walk in the park. And if the environment is so polluted that they can't do that, then that's problematic for them, for the country, and for the world.

Malik Rahim: Oh, yes.

MM: Yeah. When I saw your work on the environment, I was saying to myself that that's a good place to start. Why did you think that's an important thing out of everything that's going on in the world? What does the environment play in our struggle?

MR: My brother, there's nothing, absolutely nothing more important than us working to save our environment. We could have as many rights as any Caucasian, we could be as rich as Trump or any of the other billionaires; It won't mean a thing if we can't breathe this air or drink this water. There's nothing more important than that. Listen, I'll be seventy-six in December. What it is, fifty years from now when those kids ask their parents, what was so important that you didn't act to save this environment? What are you going to tell them?

Look at the legacy we going to leave; Right now, we're over $30 trillion in debt, we cause at least one-third of the world's pollution, and we have an arsenal of weapons of mass destruction that will be antiquated in fifty years. Where are you going to put them? You can't put them all on the Navajo Nation, so what are you going to do with them? If nothing will happen today, how much toxins are going to be in the environment in fifty years? Our rivers, lakes, and streams; think how polluted they'll be. How much plastic is going to be in our oceans if we refuse to act? And you see, the responsibility is right now in our hands. There's no place on this planet that has more institutions of higher learning than we have here in America. No place.

MM: Okay, let me ask you this here, Malik. We recognize

that in Flint, Michigan, we still have issues with the water in the community. We know that to be a fact. Prior to the Love Canal and them dumping toxic waste and getting caught—not dumping it but getting caught doing it—did we get the environmental protection. But why do you think that we have such resistance when it's self-evident what the end is going to be? It don't make no difference what capitalist, fascists, and imperialists think; In the end, you're either going to be in the spaceship in another hemisphere or another atmosphere or you're going to be subjected to the same thing as everybody else. So why do you think we have this resistance to, whenever we raise environmental issues in this country, we have a pushback from fascists saying, oh no, there ain't no such thing as global warming. No, that's fake news, fake—

MR: Because of our arrogance. Our arrogance. Nobody wants to admit that they were wrong. And listen, there's enough blame to go around for everyone. How can you blame British Petroleum or Shell when you're using their product? So, there's enough blame for us all. The time now has long passed for the blame game. Now we got to act, we got to put down all our differences and come together to save life as we know it on this planet, because that's what's at stake. If we don't do anything in the next fifty years, how much pollution is going to be in the atmosphere? And where are we going to get drinkable water? Listen, this is the only time in human history that I have ever heard when man has been able to flush down his feces with clean, drinkable water. We do it in America and don't think a thing about it. You dig? So, what's going to happen in fifty years? Even in prison?

MM: —Yeah, I got you.

MR: We flush down our feces like it ain't nothing with drinkable water and that's what almost a third of our planet's population is dying for. So again, we have to get our act together. As I said, bro, we have too many institutions of higher learning that if we could come together and form some solidarity movement on how we're going to work together to save our environment, then we could be leading the world in recovery on what can we do. I don't think we're going to stop climate change. I believe that we tipped the scale too far to stop it, but we could slow it down. We could slow it down and maybe our children or our grandchildren can find a way.

But right now, it is time for us to act because I'm going to tell you something, you're going to explain to your child why you didn't do anything but you were able to run to a Baltimore Ravens football game that you thought that was a little bit more important than saving our environment. Or a Beyoncé or Taylor Swift concert was more important than saving our environment. Because one day, we will all have to be accountable for it. And one thing about social media is it gives you the opportunity right now while nobody is in control of it, of saying not in my name. The oh no, uh-uh, you ain't going to tell me that I'm going to sit next year and elect the most powerful person on this planet, and not care about his agenda as it relates to saving life as we know it.

MM: Okay, let's look at this here then. Before we go to another subject matter, we know that in terms of this

conversation, former Vice President Al Gore—and you can weigh in on this—he carved that out as his territory in terms of educating people about the environment and the importance of the environment. And he had a worldwide platform. He was able to do a documentary on the environment and the impact of it. Why do you think that didn't have an impact in terms of making this a priority? Even today as we hear about what's going on in the world and the upcoming presidential election, or we hear about state and local elections, the environment is not on the radar.

MR: I'm going to tell you, we missed a golden opportunity with Al Gore. But that's an opportunity missed. Why are we like this? Because in America, we're so drunk on prosperity, that we can't see anything else. We would ride in a car with a person that's more drunk than us. We're electing a man who's drunk on power. So, if you got somebody that's drunk that's driving the car and you knew he was drunk and you got in the car anyway, then you have to accept the consequences. But again, it is up to us to say hey, we missed the opportunity with Al Gore, but now in 2024, we have a chance to rectify that. We have a chance to make sure that the environment is not second, third, or fourth on any political agenda. It is first because, without that, everything else is mute. Listen, I have grandkids and twenty-three great-grandkids, and I don't want to see them living in an environment where they cannot go outside and breathe fresh air.

I don't want them to be known as maybe the last generation of mankind. I don't want this for them. I don't want them to be living on a planet that's so polluted and radioactive, it's so contaminated that life expectancy is nowhere near seventy-six years. I don't want to leave that to them, where they got to clean up our mess. I don't want to see that because I'm going to tell you either they're going to love us or curse us. And it's up to us to decide whether we want to be loved by them saying, well, at least they tried to clean up the mess that they had made, or they going to curse us by saying that we stayed drunk and allowed this to happen to them, and now they got to try to clean up our mess.

MM: And speaking of mess, let's talk about what's going on in Baton Rouge and more importantly, what's going on with Proposition 3. Are you familiar with them trying to build this new jail that's glass-enclosed, circular style?

MR: And it's something that not even the sheriff wants. But we're going to force this on. Why? Because it's holding us, because you got to remember, Dixiecrats are alive and well in Louisiana. I call it Lousy-ana. So, in Lousy-ana, it is alive and well. Listen, this year we had a $200 million surplus that we could have used on crime abatement, on establishing a reentry program. We could have used it on any of the pressing problems that we face in this state, but we chose not to. We chose to give it to different politicians for their pet projects. So again, we have to change that here. We elected a governor; he won in a landslide because we didn't get out there and vote.

But then you ask yourself, why should we vote? In order to make a person do something, you have to give them a reason to do it, either out of fear or out of hope. We didn't supply either, so nobody would go. So again, when you have a state that has a 30%-plus African-American population, which adds up to about a third, but we only have one congressional seat when we should have two, when living in a state that has a $50 billion budget in this state of less than 5 million people, and close to 35% is living below the poverty line, something is wrong.

MM: Something is wrong with that pitch.

MR: How can you justify that? Listen, the actors just came off a strike. So now, once again, they're going to be making movies in this community, because we got three movie studios right here in the African American community that have priced our community out of our reach. We're already not making anything but half of what the average white person makes. Then they came into our community and now you can't even pay rent. You can't even afford to rent on the average Black salary. They took to our community, and they don't do anything for us. Listen, you would have had movies that come here that if you would add how much they earned combined, they have made, I would say close to about $15-$20 billion.

MM: Ain't never going back to the community.

MR: Ain't giving a dime. You know what it's like, my brother?

MM: What's that?

MR: It's like you telling me you think that you are going to come into my house and sell drugs and then you don't even want to get me high.

MM: Yeah.

MR: You are telling me that—

MM: You got to pay for yours, you got to pay for yours.

MR: —But you're in my house.

MM: Your house, yeah, but you got to pay for the product.

MR: Right, and that's something that doesn't compute. Either you're going to kick the table over yourself or you're going to set me up, but you're going to do something because you ain't going to let nobody abuse you like that. That's what we are doing. That's what's happening. See, they are coming off a strike, and as soon as they come off strike—because while they were on strike, we had a reprieve—now the clock is ticking again. They're coming back. They're coming back because that's all they got to do, is move in and say that now they're a citizen of Lousy-ana and they get all the benefits of being a citizen of Lousy-ana. And that means that it pushes us out of this city, and that's their plan, to push us out to New Orleans East. In New Orleans, that's our Soweto, because we couldn't stay in Johannesburg, we could stay in Soweto.

MM: Yeah, township.

MR: But see, that's the first place that'd be hit if a hurricane came.

MM: Yeah. So, they make sure one way or the other, they're going to get rid of us, huh?

MR: We're out there.

MM: Let's move forward, let's talk about the biggest plantation probably in the country: Angola. What's going on down in Angola? We shouldn't hear anything about Attica. We shouldn't hear anything. We shouldn't be hearing

anything about them renovating San Quentin. That's like them saying they're renovating Alcatraz and turning it back into a plantation on the island. We shouldn't be hearing about these places other than they've been abolished, but now we're hearing that men of Angola have got to a point where they have to actually literally file a lawsuit against the inhumane treatment of the work conditions and more importantly, the living conditions in Angola. We're talking about 2024. You never hear about this until it gets to a critical mass. Why is that?

MR: Again, it is very hard to wake somebody who's pretending to be asleep. They get away with it because we allow them to get away with it. Listen, my brother-in-law just got out of prison. He did fifty years. I have a friend of mine that I was raised with, he just came home from doing forty-seven years. So, I know too many guys that went in as young men and are coming out as old men. What they say is well, we allowed them out now because now they've entered criminal menopause. They ain't going to commit no more crime. So, we will let them out, and when we let them out, they cease to be a state problem but now they could become a federal problem. Why? As soon as they get out, the first thing we do, we hook them up on SSI so that they can get food stamps.
MM: And a stipend.

MR: Yeah, and the Section 8 housing and the old debt camp, but now that's all on federal. And then Louisiana, you got to pay a parole supervision fee. So, you find that these old guys will pay that parole supervision fee. These youngsters are telling them, man, I ain't paying you no fee for you to watch over me, but these old guys will pay it. And so again, it is no longer a burden on this state, and this state doesn't care what's a burden on this nation.

MM: Yeah. Death by a thousand cuts, huh?

MR: Oh, yes. But see, that's upon us because we allow this to happen. I'll tell you what, it couldn't have happened in our fathers' generation. And if they could have stood up, then we should stand up. We need to get our act together, but we'll never get our act together as long as we are surviving on basic instincts. That's all we want to do, is make money. If you don't think that's a problem, let a person pass and see how the family squabbles on their resources. So again, it's upon us. It's upon us to get our act together, and it doesn't take everybody. See, many of us are under the concept that it takes everybody, but it doesn't. It will only take a few of us to become the nucleus of change and that's what we got to develop. Now, again, that nucleus, we had it when the UNIA, the Universal Negro Improvement Association under the Honorable Marcus Garvey, we had it then, and I'm not talking about back to Africa.

I'm talking about how to survive American fascism because you got to remember, that after World War I, we had the most racist president that ever held the office in America, and I'm talking about Woodrow Wilson. Look at the summer of 1919 and see what they thought when we were battling the Spanish Flu and they said that Black veterans were coming back infected with the Spanish Flu. Look at what we were going through. And then in 1929 when they had the crashed market, when that happened, but we was able to survive it. Why? Because we were able to come together and organize. Now, they wouldn't give the Honorable Marcus Garvey any credit. They ran him out of the country after they had imprisoned him. But he was the reason why we survived the depression.

MM: Let me ask you this here—I see where you at with your analysis—but how do you address that fascism is more advanced, it's more fluid, it's more deceiving, it's more deceptive that, just like you said earlier, we find ourselves in gentrified neighborhoods, that we find ourselves below the poverty level? It's systemic. What do you say about the pressure and oppression that's being inflicted on people in this generation, this time of day, is far more severe and more cunning, it's designed to keep people in an ignorant state. It's designed to keep people in a drug stupor. It's designed to keep all people below the poverty level. You can be Black, white, red, or indifferent, it's designed—

MR: Understand this, my brother. It's no longer having an impact on the majority. The majority is reaping the benefits. I would say less than 30% of the American population is doing bad, that 70% is doing good, and they ain't worrying about what's happening to that 30%. And then that 30% helps support that 70% because if you look at where a person is located. There aren't that many in San Quentin, like San Quentin in the country, because San Quentin is located in one of the richest counties in California: Marin. But you don't find that in most places. In most places, they'll put a prison in a place that is struggling. And next thing you know, the prison becomes the economic anchor in that community that's fueled by outsiders. And it's not their children going to prison, it's our children going to prison, so they love it.

But we need to remember though that the Thirteenth Amendment that abolished slavery always had that exception clause, and that exception clause is the reason why right now we could be enslaved. Right now, especially as African Americans, because when you look at us as the African American male population, it's almost 40% of us are caught up in some way in the criminal justice system. So again, that's the way we are caught up, and we haven't looked at. . . . Listen, if a person tells me, hey, man, I ain't got no money to help you get on your feet but if you commit a crime, I'm going to throw the book at you and I'm going to spend whatever it takes to lock you up for the rest of your life, and then he has his hand out in friendship, you'll be a damned fool if you shake his hand.

MM: —Yeah, throw the rock and hide the hand now.

MR: Yeah. Man, listen, we got to do better than this. That's the thing that the Black Panther Party was built around. That's what it was centered around. You think we have to build that same. It not only happened with the Honorable Marcus Garvey because you got to remember, he and a sister named Henrietta Davis came together and formed the Black Cross Nurses, which saved us during the Spanish flu. All right.

And then when you go back in time and you look at what the Honorable Elijah Muhammad did to help save our community, to help us start seeing, these are our successes. Not failures. These are successes where they took the bottom core, that 30%, that 10% of us that was living in abject poverty and gave us hope by giving us something to stand on. Then you go up to the Honorable Minister Farrakhan, I'm seeing him go to LA and made the Crips and the Bloods sign a truce that they were going to end this nonsense of killing each other over colors and allowed us to lose Los Angeles because we had Los Angeles, but we Cripped our way and Blooded our way out of it. So again, when you see a man that's doing this and they won't give him a venue that has proven success in public housing. Now again, I always look at this, and I know I might step on somebody's toes when I say it.

MM: If they out there, they might get them out the way then.

MR: In Chicago, that's where President Obama came from; the most powerful man in the country, one of the most powerful men in the world if not the most powerful man in the world when he was the President of the United States. Oprah Winfrey is out of Chicago, one of the richest Black women in the world and one that has more influence than any other Black woman in the country. And you have Minister Farrakhan and all of them in this coming out of the same community of Chicago, and it's the murder capital.

MM: You left one out. They were killed for a pair of tennis shoes.

MR: Oh, yeah. Listen, if you have that much power and influence in one city, it shouldn't be anything but a model of success. Now if it's failing there, then why should I take the time when those three then found some reason that they can't work together? Two of them can, but they ain't from public housing. They ain't dealing with the projects. But then you have somebody that has success in going and ending the violence, not only in public housing but in this country, and you don't want him to come to the table. Now I'm saying, I'm not a member of the Nation of Islam but I got to always give credit where credit is due.

MM: As we close out, what are you doing now? What'd you want our audience to know? Some of the work, what you're doing there, and how they can participate in your endeavors.

MR: Oh, my brother, listen, one of the things that I completed, a successful fifty-seventh celebration of the Black Panther Party.

MM: All right, all power to the people.

MR: We completed that because in October, we call it Black Panther Month, and so for the fifty-seventh anniversary we gave a celebration here at five different venues that was successful. So, that's what we are doing right now. General Rico Forbes, the former president of the Republic of New Africa, and I have come together and we have formed a group called Global Solidarity Network where we're willing to network with anybody that's talking about environmental peace and justice. Every Monday, Wednesday, and Friday at four o'clock, I do a podcast on Facebook. I do a Facebook Live for an hour from 4 to 5, and that's every Monday, Wednesday, and Friday where I speak about these things. So, they could listen in.

But the main thing is to get involved in your community wherever you're at. That's how you could help me, by doing something wherever you're at. I don't say that you got to wait till you get in touch with me, because you might never get in touch with me, for you to act. Do something in your community and then we can network. We can network because we have this medium and right now this is the only medium that nobody can control. I'm going to tell you, every day they trying to figure out a way that they could shut this down.

MM: You better know it.

MR: They don't want to hear anybody talking about rattling the bars. When you rattle the bars, that means them folks coming out. So again, they don't want to see this. They don't want to see this so what we got to do, we got to take advantage of it, while it's alive. We got to beat the iron while it's hot. There's an old street saying that we say here: The shade of a toothpick beat the hot, burning sun. So, we got to start off in that little shade until we work our way up, until next thing you know, we under the tree, but we got to get there. So, the thing that I'm doing and will do all the way up until the most high calls me home, is to ring the bell. It's to be a seed planter. Let them know, hey, man, listen. I work under the premise, my brother, that you can overcome any obstacle if you do three things: Put your faith in God, your confidence in yourself, and be willing to make a sacrifice.

MM: There you have it.

MR: If you do those three, you have it because if you're laying up there on somebody else's morals, you're living off a handout from somebody else, then one day that handout ain't going to be there, so you got to learn how to do for self. That's why in the party, we used to call it a self-sufficiency program, a survival program. That's why I was saying, if you look at the example, the UNIA, how it saved us from a Great Depression, from dealing with a pandemic. We was able to do it by doing it for ourself.

We have that ability, we got to start doing it. Like I said, it ain't going to take everybody. As a survivor of the Civil Rights and the Black Power Movement, I know that it was less than 3% of us that participated in the Civil Rights Movement. You hear today everybody talking about, yeah, man. I was in the Civil Rights Movement, and I say, wow, if you were, what happened? And then when you get to the Black Power Movement, less than 2% of us actually participated in the Black Power Movement. But now you find thousands of Panthers. My daddy was in the Panther Party, my uncle was in the Panther Party, my auntie, my mama, everybody was in the party. But if everybody would've been in the party, we wouldn't have lost, we would've won. So again, what we have to do, we got to give our life some meaning. And I'm going to tell you something, ain't nothing more meaningful than to say that I fought on the cause of saving life as we know it on this planet. There's nothing more noble than to say that I was involved in the struggle for environmental peace and justice.

About Mansa Musa

Mansa Musa, also known as Charles Hopkins, is a seventy-year-old social activist and former Black Panther. He was released from prison on December 5, 2019, after serving forty-eight years, nine months, five days, sixteen hours, and ten minutes. He cohosts the TRNN original show Rattling the Bars.

For Further Reading

The Angola 3
King, Robert Hillary. *From the Bottom of the Heap: The Autobiography of Black Panther Robert Hillary King*. Oakland, CA: PM Press, 2012.

Woodfox, Albert. *Solitary*. New York, NY: HarperCollins, 2021.

The Black Panther Party for Self-Defense
Alkebulan, Paul. *Survival Pending Revolution: The History of the Black Panther Party*. Tuscaloosa: The University of Alabama Press, 2007.

Arend, Orissa. *Showdown in Desire: The Black Panthers Take a Stand in New Orleans*. Fayetteville: University of Arkansas Press, 2010.

Brown, Elaine. *A Taste of Power: A Black Woman's Story*. New York: Knopf, 2015.

Ismail, Malik. *From Old Guard to Vanguard: A 2nd Generation Panther* (Second Edition). Create Space Independent Publishing, 2017.

Murch, Donna Jean. *Living for the City: Migration, Education, and the Rise of the Black Panther Party in Oakland, California.* Chapel Hill: University of North Carolina Press, 2010.

Nelson, Alondra. *Body and Soul: The Black Panther Party and the Fight against Medical Discrimination.* Minneapolis: University of Minnesota Press, 2011.

Newton, Huey P. *The Huey P. Newton Reader.* New York: Seven Stories Press, 2002.

Sonnie, Amy and Tracy, James. *Hillbilly Nationalists, Urban Race Rebels, and Black Power—Updated and Revised: Interracial Solidarity in 1960s–70s New Left Organizing.* New York: Melville House, 2021.

Common Ground Relief

crow, scott. *Black Flags and Windmills: Hope, Anarchy, and the Common Ground Collective.* Oakland, CA: PM Press, 2014.

Mutual Aid & Community Resilience

Dunson, Jimmy. *Building Power When the Lights Are Out: Disasters, Mutual Aid and Dual Power.* Tampa, FL: Rebel Hearts Publishing, 2022.

Fithian, Lisa. *Shut It Down: Stories from a Fierce, Loving Resistance.* New York: Chelsea Green Publishing, 2019.

Solnit, Rebecca. *Hope in the Dark: Untold Histories, Wild Possibilities.* Chicago, IL: Haymarket Books, 2016.

Spade, Dean. *Mutual Aid: Building Solidarity During This Crisis (and the Next).* New York: Verso, 2020.

HOPE VI and Public Housing

Baranski, John. *Housing the City by the Bay: Tenant Activism, Civil Rights, and Class Politics in San Francisco.* Palo Alto, CA: Stanford University Press, 2019.

Howard, Amy. *More Than Housing: Activism and Community in San Francisco Public Housing.* Minneapolis: University of Minnesota, 2014.

Tracy, James. *Dispatches Against Displacement: Field Notes from San Francisco's Housing Wars.* Oakland, CA: AK Press, 2014.

Williams, Rhonda. *The Politics of Public Housing: Black Women's Struggles against Urban Inequality.* Oxford, UK: Oxford University Press, 2004.

Acknowledgments

This book is dedicated to the members of the New Orleans Black Panther Party, the International Committee to Free the Angola 3 and volunteers of the original Common Ground Relief.

Salute! Verilin Dampeer, Juliette Torrez, General Rico Forbes, Zach Blue, Angelica Sgouros, Orissa Arend, Rebecca Solnit, scott crow, Todd Sanchioni, Scott Fleming, jackie summell, Rain, and Marina Drummer.

Legacy Left

Legacy Left publishes pocketbooks that asks movement veterans the question, "What do you want to pass on to the next generation?"

AK Press

AK Press is a worker self-managed publisher and distributor and that specializing in books about the radical left and anarchism.